CENTRE FOR EDUCATION RESEARCH

Our Children at Risk

ORGANISATION FOR ECONOMIC CO-OPERATION AND DEVELOPMENT

ORGANISATION FOR ECONOMIC CO-OPERATION AND DEVELOPMENT

Pursuant to Article 1 of the Convention signed in Paris on 14th December 1960, and which came into force on 30th September 1961, the Organisation for Economic Co-operation and Development (OECD) shall promote policies designed:

— to achieve the highest sustainable economic growth and employment and a rising standard of living in Member countries, while maintaining financial stability, and thus to contribute to the development of the world economy;

— to contribute to sound economic expansion in Member as well as non-member countries in the process of economic development; and

— to contribute to the expansion of world trade on a multilateral, non-discriminatory basis in accordance with international obligations.

The original Member countries of the OECD are Austria, Belgium, Canada, Denmark, France, Germany, Greece, Iceland, Ireland, Italy, Luxembourg, the Netherlands, Norway, Portugal, Spain, Sweden, Switzerland, Turkey, the United Kingdom and the United States. The following countries became Members subsequently through accession at the dates indicated hereafter: Japan (28th April 1964), Finland (28th January 1969), Australia (7th June 1971), New Zealand (29th May 1973) and Mexico (18th May 1994). The Commission of the European Communities takes part in the work of the OECD (Article 13 of the OECD Convention).

The Centre for Educational Research and Innovation was created in June 1968 by the Council of the Organisation for Economic Co-operation and Development and all Member countries of the OECD are participants.

The main objectives of the Centre are as follows:

— *to promote and support the development of research activities in education and undertake such research activities where appropriate;*

— *to promote and support pilot experiments with a view to introducing and testing innovations in the educational system;*

— *to promote the development of co-operation between Member countries in the field of educational research and innovation.*

The Centre functions within the Organisation for Economic Co-operation and Development in accordance with the decisions of the Council of the Organisation, under the authority of the Secretary-General. It is supervised by a Governing Board composed of one national expert in its field of competence from each of the countries participating in its programme of work.

Publié en français sous le titre :
LES ENFANTS A RISQUE

Foreword

Children "at risk" are estimated to include up to 30 per cent of school age children in some OECD countries and the challenges that they present have become key policy questions. The concerns stem, not only from the claims of social justice, but also from the need to develop high level skills, in as many young people as possible, in order to maintain employment, productivity levels and economic prosperity. This is a situation that is further exacerbated by the increasing number of retired citizens and the falling birth rate.

The initial outline of the study was agreed in 1989, when representatives from seventeen OECD Member countries met in Paris. They have contributed extensively to this book through country reports and case studies. In addition there have been two important international seminars supported by the US Department of Education's Office of Under Secretary, Planning and Evaluation Service. The first of these held in 1990 considered the problem in general while the second, held in 1991, focused on issues of evaluation. Three Foundations, Freudenberg, van Leer and C.S. Mott, have also been particularly supportive and have enriched the work with reports of their own research.

Chapter I of the report provides a general overview of the concept of "at risk", its prevalence and the methodology used. It goes on to discuss national policies and intervention strategies in the three areas of pre-school, school, and transition to work periods. The chapter concludes with a consideration of cross-cutting issues. Chapters II, III, and IV identify important practical issues as derived in the main from the case studies provided in the areas of pre-school, school and transition to work respectively. Chapter V provides a conclusion and also discusses policy issues.

The report has been prepared by the CERI Secretariat with the advice and contributions of experts. Professor Klaus Wedell of the Institute of Education at the University of London, UK, was the principal consultant on the study from the beginning to the end.

The report is published on the responsibility of the Secretary-General of the OECD.

Summary

This report is concerned with children and youth "at risk". It synthesises data based on country reports and case studies from 17 OECD Member countries and three foundations. The work covers issues relating to the preschool, school age and transition to work periods. Following an introductory chapter further chapters are devoted to each of these three themes. A final fifth chapter draws together the main conclusions and identifies policy issues. Each chapter is concluded by a series of key points.

The challenges presented by children and youth "at risk" have become key policy issues. The concerns stem, not only from the claims of social justice, but also from the need to develop high level skills, in as many young people as possible, in order to maintain employment and productivity levels and economic prosperity. This is a situation that is further exacerbated by the increasing number of retired citizens and the falling birth rate. Those "at risk" come from disadvantaged backgrounds, they fail to reach the necessary standards in school, often drop-out and as a consequence fail to become integrated into a normally accepted pattern of social responsibility, particularly with regard to work and adult life. There are many manifestations of a failure to integrate successfully which include: health problems, substance and drug abuse, crime, early pregnancy and unemployment. For most countries between 15 and 30 per cent of children are considered to be "at risk". Factors which predict "at risk" status include a background of poverty, ethnic minority status, features of family arrangements, e.g. single parent status, poor knowledge of the language of instruction, the type and geographical location of the school attended and community factors such as poor housing. It is important to note that risk factors can cumulate in such a way that the presence of one factor is associated with school failure with the same probability as no factor; two factors predict a four-fold, while four factors predict a ten-fold likelihood of failure.

The concept of "at risk" is an optimistic one which emphasises the importance of preventive actions at all three stages studied. This means that there is a need to develop sound preschool education planned in the light of a full understanding of the complex ways in which families from many different cultural backgrounds actually function. At school age, school organisation, curriculum and pedagogies must be flexible enough to meet the educational and social needs of children and their families and to take account of community wishes and business interests. Teachers and other staff should be adequately trained and given enough time to plan and develop their teaching and support. During the period of transition to work "at risk" students must be given high quality support and advice from a variety of informed sources in order to give them the best possible start on the labour market. Direct experience in the work place is a useful method. The successful implementation of strategies, to help those ''at risk'' succeed, also requires funding methods that give schools and local education authorities flexibility in the way resources are used. This freedom, however, needs to be fostered within a framework of co-ordinated policy development across various ministries including those concerned with education, health, social services and employment and in which evaluation is afforded a high priority and cost effectiveness determined.

Table of Contents

Chapter I

Children and Youth "at risk"

Chapter II

Programmes and Issues Related to Early Childhood

Chapter III

Changing Schools

Chapter IV

Transition from School to Work

Chapter V

Conclusions and Policy Implications

Chapter I

Children and Youth "at risk"

by

Peter Evans
Center for Educational Research and Innovation, OECD, Paris

General overview

Introduction

Children and youth "at risk" (CYAR) are those pupils from disadvantaged back-grounds who fail to reach the necessary standards in school, often drop-out and as a consequence fail to become integrated into a normally accepted pattern of social responsibility, particularly with regard to work and family life.

The matter has become an issue of urgent concern for a number of now well-known social and economic reasons. Long standing issues of social priorities remain pertinent. To these can now be added changes in the labour market which have led to demands for ever more skilled workers who can operate effectively and competitively in the increasingly complex conditions of the work place. In addition workers must increasingly show a preparedness to continue to develop and expand their skills; attitudes which must also be allied to flexibility and a willingness to consider alternative forms of employment throughout the cycle of working life.

These factors have to be set against a backdrop of substantial changes in the nature of the population of many OECD Member countries. The birth rate is declining and the number of retired people is increasing. As a consequence the proportion of citizens available to support and maintain many economies at their present level is reduced.

Taken together, these developments, if not tackled effectively, could threaten the prosperity as well as the social cohesion of many OECD Member countries. High levels of unemployment, leading to decreases in revenues, and increases in passive benefits allied to increasing costs of health care of the growing aged population are but a few of the challenging implications which are leading to wide ranging reviews of many of the accepted services in our societies.

The education system has not escaped scrutiny, since education is seen as a major force in improving skills and developing appropriate social attitudes. In this regard it is widely accepted that far too many children fail at school with social and personally tragic outcomes.

It is in the light of these menacing background factors of economic, social and humanitarian concerns that this study has been carried out. Specifically the task was to review the situation with regard to CYAR in OECD Member countries and to identify and describe innovation and effective educational practices for preschool and, school aged children and those making the transition from school to work.

Structure of the report

This report on the CERI study on CYAR brings together much of the work that has been carried out over the duration of the study. The main input has been in the form of country reports and case studies. But where relevant, this has been supplemented by other material. In addition the work has been enriched through two international conferences held in the United States where most of the participating countries were represented. The first of these, held in 1990, provided an occasion for a discussion of the broad issues concerned with CYAR. The second, held in 1991, considered methods of evaluation of intervention programmes for CYAR. In addition the work has benefited from extensive support from a number of foundations who have made further studies available to us. Three foundations have been especially supportive: the Freudenberg Foundation of Germany, the Mott Foundation of the United States and the van Leer Foundation of the Netherlands.

The report is divided into five chapters. The first, based on country reports, provides an introduction to the main aims and methods of the study and includes an account which brings together the principal issues as perceived by the participating countries. This section outlines the nature of the problem, discusses the concept of "at risk" and its prevalence. It then describes national policies and, under the heading of intervention strategies, discusses relevant issues pertaining to the phases of preschool, school and transition to work. It concludes with a section on cross-cutting issues. Matters concerned with preschool, school and transition to work are then elaborated in later chapters which provide syntheses of the case studies that were made available. The preschool chapter emphasises prevention. The chapter on schooling emphasises strategies for change and the chapter on transition to work reviews and analyses the strategies adopted in a number of OECD Member countries. A final chapter concludes the report by bringing together common themes and some of their policy implications. Each chapter is rounded off with a set of keypoints.

The chapters have been written by different authors and reflect differing amounts and quantity of data that were available. In addition they vary in style. Each one has been written to stand alone and for this reason there is, on occasion, some overlap between them.

The methodology used in the study was straight-forward. During the course of meetings of country representatives and experts in Paris a definition of the term CYAR was agreed upon. In addition frameworks for the country reports and case studies were determined. These frameworks are given in annex one. The country report comprised four major sections concerned with gathering information on:

- Who is "at risk"?
- Intervention strategies for different age groups.
- Transition to work.
- General section on cross-cutting issues.

This report was intended to provide a broad range of information on how CYAR were conceptualised by participating countries, their prevalence and the policies and practices designed to meet the perceived needs.

The case study reports were intended to provide detailed information on initiatives taken to develop effective provision for CYAR. Good practice was to be emphasised. The studies selected reflected both "top down" and "bottom up" approaches, *i.e.* programmes initiated by governments or other official agencies and community based projects that were usually wholly or partly funded by private foundations.

Descriptions of the case studies were to cover:

- The aims of the programme studied.
- The target population.
- The specific context.
- The operation of the programme and the services etc., used (including resourcing) to achieve the aims.
- The evolution of the programme.
- The evaluation of the (multiple) outcomes of the programme in relation to evolving aims, context, policy, etc.

In preparing their material, countries were asked to follow these frameworks but otherwise no additional constraints were imposed. The case studies were selected by the OECD Member countries and the foundations involved. In the event some 42 studies were received, the majority being concerned with school aged children.

The report is based on information received from 17 participating countries: Australia, Belgium, Canada, Finland, France, Germany, Greece, Ireland, Italy, Japan, the Netherlands, Portugal, Sweden, Turkey, the United Kingdom, the United States and the former Yugoslavia.

Material from the three foundations already mentioned, *i.e.* Freudenberg, Mott and van Leer, was also incorporated.

The concept of "at risk"

Some background

The term "children and youth at risk" is a relatively recent descriptor that has emerged to replace the earlier term "disadvantage". The strength of the term "at risk" lies in its future looking emphasis and by implication its stress on prevention.

The importance of thinking in terms of prevention can really not be overstated since it reflects a significant explanatory shift in the balance of factors that are believed to lead to failure both in school and social integration. The new key element is the recognition of the importance of a developmental perspective. This view implies "that 'at risk' students have certain characteristics that make it possible to identify them, but that these characteristics become problematic only in conjunction with events and conditions that have yet to unfold" (Natriello *et al.*, 1990).

But this was not always the case and a number of factors can be identified that help to put this interactive view of the concept of "at risk" into context. The need for a different interpretation of failing in school stems in general from social change over the last century which has led to our increasingly global, mobile and complex societies and economies.

Perceived needs for an educated workforce arose towards the end of the last century and have continued since. Education systems were set up in which some children were successful and some were not. However, at the time, lack of success was not seen as crucial since those who were not successful at school were absorbed onto the labour market, for instance as unskilled agricultural workers. This arrangement met the then current socio-political needs, at least for an adult workforce.

From their inception schools have performed a sorting function. In the first instance many significant decisions were based on teachers' judgements. But it became clear that although ability to learn (as perceived by teachers) was based partly on intelligence it was also influenced by other less important factors such as social skills, appearance and docility. In Paris, Binet was given the task of helping schools to identify pupils who would be unable to profit from the schooling offered. This was to be based on objective assessment and intended to prevent less relevant factors being used to place children, unjustly, in special schools because, for instance, the teacher was unable to cope with the child's uniqueness.

This approach was stimulated by a number of other developments. There was a growing interest in statistics and anthropometry, and from this the idea of a normal statistical distribution of intelligence was developed. This idea supported by Darwinian inheritance theory, led to the notion of the heritability of human traits. Such a view persists strongly to this day and the idea of the fixed intelligence quotient (IQ) that derived from this period is still popular and widely believed in – although less so by social scientists.

This view remained highly influential in education until the 1960s when both theoretical and empirical analyses challenged the generalisation of the idea of fixed intelligence and by the late 1960s it was being realised that both genetic and environmental factors were of importance in determining individual adaptation (for a definitive review see Rutter and Madge, 1976). Lest the influence of this analysis may seem overstated, it is worth remembering that as late as 1971 Simon argued that one of the reasons why effective pedagogy had not developed for the slow learner, at least in the United Kingdom, was because of the belief in fixed levels of ability such as the IQ which led teachers to conclude that nothing much could be done for these children.

Also at this time in many OECD Member countries there was great social change. Many countries witnessed immigration from the former colonies on a large scale and began to come to grips with the implications of increased heterogeneity of the population. The new ethnic minorities posed considerable problems for education services for they came with quite different cultural backgrounds. At the same time the learning difficulties of many children from the indigenous population began to be seen in terms of cultural deprivation and social disadvantage; terms which emphasised family, personal and social factors in development, e.g. Havighurst (1965). Various authors amplified these issues. For instance Bernstein (1975) stressed the importance of different codes used by middle class and lower class families which influence patterns of communication and interactions and ultimately their impact on cognitive development and their ability to benefit equally from schooling. Kohn and Schooler (1985) identified different attitudinal patterns. Independence was seen as typifying middle class families which was to be contrasted with working class patterns of conformity that were seen to limit educational attainment and aspiration. Bourdieu (1984) likewise identified differences in life style related to class which influences the growth of cultural capital in the family. Schooling can expand on cultural capital but cannot compensate entirely for lack of such experiences within the family.

The difficulties and attitudinal dispositions referred to above led to the notion of educational disadvantage which emphasised difficulties in learning caused by social or cultural characteristics and educational deprivation, whereby the normal school facilities are available to many pupils only in a restricted form (Passow, 1970).

In contrast, others have argued that those from lower socio-economic strata and who might be considered disadvantaged, in fact possess a culture of their own and are therefore different but not deficient. Furthermore, the finding that many pupils from the same community achieved perfectly well did not fit neatly into a cultural or educational deprivation theory. In addition, Baratz and Baratz (1970) argued that the concept of cultural deprivation could all too easily lead to institutionalised racism whereby children and youth who are referred to as disadvantaged are in fact the product of wider economic processes at work which leads to distinctions that schools serve merely to reproduce.

The orientations, discussed briefly above, serve as useful background pointers to understanding the link between disadvantage and failure but their generalisation is limited mainly because terms such as ''working class'' conceal huge differences in attitudes and behaviour on the part of the members of the group. In addition, as will be seen, the notion of ''at risk'' includes those from ethnic minority groups where educational problems are complicated by different patterns of child rearing, different home language and attitudes to schooling and this further clouds the picture.

The idea that it is better to describe disadvantaged pupils as "at risk" has developed from this background. The term "at risk" emphasises future prospects. It is a predictive concept which assumes that children and pupils "at risk" have certain characteristics which allow them to be identified but that these characteristics only become a problem when they meet events and conditions that have yet to occur. Stodolsky and Lesser (1967) for example have argued that the time has come to go beyond definitions of "at risk" which are based on characteristics such as social class, ethnicity and poverty towards definitions which incorporate the "environmental circumstances which are closely articulated with developmental processes and which vary considerably within and across social class and ethnic lines". In other words the search is on for explanatory factors which have a direct impact on learning and which in turn can be manipulated.

This view of "at risk" does not search for causes solely in the school, the family or the community but may link all three. For instance Levin (1986) has argued that "people defined as educationally disadvantaged (or "at risk") lack the home and community resources to fully benefit from recent educational reforms as well as from conventional school practices".

The term "at risk" is not without its critics. It does not, for instance, translate well into French where the term "a risque" tends to imply within child difficulties – clearly a meaning not carried by the concept when used in an *educational* context in English, although it has been pointed out that the association of the term with *health care* encourages a within child view. Others [*e.g.* Freedberg (1987)] have expressed concern about the effects of labelling minority groups for instance as "at risk" that may well create and perpetuate racial stereotypes. It is argued that such labels have handicapped minority groups over many years, leading to watered down educational experiences and low expectations. Furthermore given that the term "at risk" is predictive, and implies that it is possible to guess how students will progress in the future, it could create problems for students who would otherwise not have had them – outcomes which can again lead to self-fulfilling prophecies. These arguments have a long history and they relate to the general difficulty of how to get additional resources to those in need without, at the same time, stigmatising them. An issue which the present study does not address directly.

Since work has been underway in CERI, for many years, that has focused on the disabled, it was agreed at the outset that the term "at risk" would be limited to those students who come from disadvantaged families and who do not show any obvious predisposing physical impairments likely to categorise them as disabled. Funding arrangements for the disabled and those "at risk" also emanate from different sources. The target group are those children whose learning and adjustment problems have their origin in factors in the social environment which, over time, may cumulatively develop into "within-child" variables and which are associated with difficulties in learning and adapting to the school and its curriculum and ultimately to the normally accepted demands of society. Both the disabled and those "at risk" have difficulties in learning. However, the perceived main "cause" is different, being physical in the former and social in the latter.

It is also clear that some children who are said to be "at risk" demonstrate a resilience and are successful both in school and in life. Although little appears to be known about the factors that develop resilience, it nevertheless remains important to emphasise that the fact that some children do show resilience does *not* invalidate the need to deal with negative environmental conditions.

The purpose of the all too brief discussion above has been to show that the concept of "at risk" has emerged relatively recently from a background which has sought to demonstrate that certain groups of people have a greater propensity than others for educational failure. Over time the balance of the scientific argument has shifted from differences which emphasised "within-child" variables, such as inherited intelligence, or "within-group" variables such as child rearing practices said to discriminate between middle and working class groups, to those which focus on the appropriate adaptation of individuals.

The concept of "at risk" becomes an optimistic one if it moves the debate foreword by recognising the transactional nature of much learning. In the educational context this means that the right educational experiences over time can help to compensate for disadvantage and optimise the chances of success of all pupils.

However, it must be recognised that schooling is only one influence on children's development and for this reason can play only a limited part in their education. Under this argument effective education necessitates bringing together the school, the family and the community. Those "at risk" are likely to have had unsatisfactory experiences in one or more of these areas.

Non-school factors relating to school failure

Schorr (1988) has described some of the non-school factors that could have pre-natal, peri-natal and post-natal sequelae, which would relate to school failure and adolescent problems, including delinquency, and which would need compensatory actions. These are:

- growing up in persistent or concentrated poverty and in a family of low social class;
- being born unwanted or into a family with too many children born too close together;
- growing up with a parent who is unemployed, a teenager, a school drop-out, or illiterate, a parent who is impaired (as a result of alcoholism, drug addiction, or mental illness), and/or a parent who is without social supports;
- growing up in a family or neighbourhood with such a high level of social disorganisation as to leave a young child unprotected from abuse and violence, and with little exposure to healthy role models;
- growing up outside one's family, especially in multiple foster care or institutional placements; and
- growing up with the sense that one has bleak prospects for good employment or a stable family life and little power to affect one's own destiny and that one is not valued by the outside world.

Multiplicative effect of risk factors

Risk factors also have a pernicious multiplying effect. Rutter (1980) found that children suffering from one risk factor were likely to experience serious consequences with the same probability as those with no risk factors. However, if two or three risk factors were present the chances of an unfavourable outcome increased four times. With four risk factors the chances of a negative outcome increased by ten times.

The concept of "at risk" as described by OECD Member countries

It is clear that there is substantial agreement among OECD Member countries about the general nature of who is "at risk". A few countries located the concept quite specifically within a policy framework of equality. In Australia, an objective of social justice requires fair and equitable access to resources. In Greece those "at risk" lack equal educational opportunities and in Sweden social policy objectives identify those "at risk" as being excluded from participation, influence and work. The United States notes its historic commitment to greater opportunity for all groups. Although other countries did not specifically mention the concept within the general framework of the goals of social democracy and pluralism, it is unlikely that any would demur.

More detailed considerations of "at risk" lied in the understanding of the concept, to paraphrase the Belgian report, as an active expression of a preventive idea. Given this basic assumption, the sort of explanatory factors that will emerge are bound to focus on predictive variables: they will focus on the identification of potential individuals "at risk" of developing problems and learning difficulties given an exposure to certain adverse conditions. Identifying these factors then provides the possibility of describing chains of events which are open to change through environmental modification and which may be used in a description of "causes".

Despite agreement that the work should focus on the disadvantaged, some countries were unable to exclude at least some children with disabilities, particularly the physically and mentally handicapped. Those children who have disabilities of this sort are patently "at risk". However, the distinction between social and physical precursors of failure noted earlier is maintained and the report concentrates on the issues of social disadvantage. In practice, the issue is not however as clear cut as this description would imply since many countries see educational problems best described as being on a continuum of "need". In this case the term most frequently used is "special educational needs" and this cuts across the divide between disability and "at risk". The failure of the pupil to learn effectively in school is a key underlying concept that unites the two descriptions and if the problem is perceived in this way then the terms "at risk" and "special educational needs", are essentially co-terminous. However, for most countries the terms "at risk" and handicap are kept distinct.

As determined from the country reports the following paragraphs elaborate the concept of "at risk" under the following headings:

- an operational definition;
- economic consequences;
- predictive factors;
- manifestations of school failure;
- manifestations of social failure;
- a systems framework;
- breaking away; and
- gender.

An operational definition

An operational definition may be distilled from the country reports as follows: children and youth "at risk" are viewed as those failing in school and unsuccessful in making the transition to work and adult life and as a consequence are unlikely to be able to make a full contribution to active society.

Economic consequences

A whole range of economic consequences follow such as the costs to social security, health and social services and lost tax revenues as well as productivity. These issues have been discussed in other OECD reports such as in the CERI project on multicultural education (OECD, 1991) and in the activity on access participation and equity (OECD, 1993). However, in recent years the OECD has not undertaken comparative studies. The financial implications are likely to be substantial, however. For instance, it has been estimated (conservatively) that the cost of maintaining disabled people under the age of 30 in the United States (a much smaller population), on passive lifelong total dependency programmes, is in excess of $1 trillion (Gerry, 1992).

Predictive factors

A number of predictive factors have been identified that are strongly associated with failure as noted above. The term "predictive" has been chosen carefully, and does not imply direct causation. The "predictive factors" that were identified were as follows:

Poverty

- poverty concentration of a school – in schools with high proportions of children from poor families there tends to be low academic performance and high drop-out;
- family poverty status – in the United States students from low income families are twice as likely as high income students to perform in the lowest quartile on standardised achievement tests; and
- duration of poverty – those who live in families that are poor for a long period of time are more likely to fall behind than those living in poverty for a short period.

Ethnic minority status and aboriginality (Australia)

In many OECD countries, children with ethnic minority status are more likely to show low school achievement, to drop out and to become unemployed. However, there are some important qualifications to this statement.

First, there are many different ethnic minorities, indigenous groups as well as immigrants. In addition there are groups of travellers, *e.g.* gypsies, or circus families, whose children may not attend school consistently.

Second, different groups show different characteristics. Thus in inner city areas in the United Kingdom, children from some Asian countries show higher school attainments than the "native" population, a finding at variance with the performance of immigrant groups overall.

Finally, second and third generation immigrants tend to achieve higher standards, and girls often fare better than boys. In short, although ethnic minority status may be a generally good predictor of educational under-performing, there are many exceptions.

Family issues

Family issues rank high in the reports as being strongly associated with "at risk" status. A number of aspects have been identified:
- One parent families: these may be either permanent, temporary or transient. A high proportion of school aged children live permanently with one parent (approximately 25 per cent in the United States) and this arrangement is linked with lower achievement levels. Such families are often also poor and it is probably this factor acting in association with others, which correlate with lower educational achievement. Providing appropriate financial support gives the freedom to allow parents to contribute.
- There are also temporary arrangements that occur. Fathers may be immigrant workers and working elsewhere in another country but would return home from time to time. Some may be merchant sailors, some in prison.
- Transient families whereby second adults may come and go are also not infrequent.
- There is evidence that level of family education is associated with "at risk" status in some countries. In the Netherlands for instance, additional resources are provided to schools for children who come from such families.
- Housing: some families lack adequate housing and some children may effectively have no home at all.
- Home-school breakdown: this factor was mentioned by a number of countries as being very strongly associated with "at risk" status. Frequently families do not support the goals of the school. In some cases it was argued that the children themselves do not see the school as being relevant. It is too abstract. Real learning takes place in the workplace.
- Child abuse: this factor is also associated with poor school performance.

Any of these conditions may lead to extreme family stress of one sort or another with the potential of associated psychosomatic symptoms such as depression. The idea of families living in stressful conditions or being stressed was noted by Turkey as a factor which led to "at risk" status.

Poor knowledge of the majority language

Inadequate knowledge of the language of instruction is associated with low attainment. The improvement of school performance in second and third generation immigrants, noted above, may well be partly explained by improvements on the part of the immigrants in the adopted country's language of instruction.

Type of school

The type of school, *e.g.* government, independent or denominational, was seen by some countries as an important variable since some schools outperformed others in terms of achievement levels. Classroom factors are also of considerable significance.

Geography

The location in which the education was taking place was also seen as a potentially limiting factor. In Australia, fewer pupils are reported to complete schooling in rural in contrast to urban areas, although recent studies in that country have shown that a simple urban/rural dichotomy ignores variations within these generalised localities.

Community factors

Poor housing, a lack of community support, the non-availability and non-use of leisure facilities and the lack of political resources were also seen as predictive of "at risk" status.

In determining "at risk" outcomes all of these factors may work together or in isolation. But what emerges in general is the idea of a lack of stimulation leading to decreased cultural capital that can come about as a result of a large number of routes. The global and correlative nature of these factors should be noted as well as the fact that they work interactively. Thus at this stage, although they can be used predictively, it is not possible to derive specific casual connections.

Manifestations of school failure

The manifestations of school failure are well known and are listed below:
- low attainment;
- low satisfaction and self-esteem;
- lack of participation;
- truancy;
- school refusal;
- drop-out;

23

- behaviour problems (aggression in boys, careless approach to risk of early pregnancy in girls); and
- delinquency.

Manifestations of social failure

The factors noted in the preceding paragraphs are associated with various levels of marginalisation. Some of the behavioural manifestations of this for youth include:
- health problems;
- substance abuse and use of drugs;
- psycho-somatic illness;
- early pregnancy;
- inability to integrate into work and unemployment;
- poverty; and
- crime.

A systems framework

In general terms, countries recognised the need to understand the problems presented by CYAR within a broadly conceived systems framework where many of life events experienced by children taken singly or together can lead to future educational difficulty. In addition, some of the country reports noted the importance of appreciating a developmental or transactional dimension to the problem and the importance of recognising that events cumulate over time while interacting with constitutional factors within the child. The United Kingdom report noted the way in which events can link in a chain leading to success or failure. For instance low socio-economic factors may lead to poor socialisation patterns in the home leading to a poor attitude by the child to school, leading in its turn to relative failure. Thus this description agrees well with that derived from research literature.

Within the understanding noted above and with our current state of knowledge, it is clearly impossible to identify the necessary and sufficient conditions that cause children to develop adaptational difficulties. In the present state of knowledge, the most promising course of action is to develop broad co-ordinated programmes intended to improve conditions for as many children and families as possible based on what is known about the effects of the range of factors identified above on the successful development of children.

Breaking away

Not much was said in the reports about the factors that lead to children overcoming adversity or why some children are apparently resilient. Although constitutional factors may be important, the factor identified as most significant was support in the family or the support of some identified person. Stability in the child's life is therefore given some focus. Schools were seen by some countries as having an important role to play, in this respect, not only in terms of emotional support but also in providing visions of the future for the child, *e.g.* some idea of the potential sort of work in business and other organisations, for example in management, as well as a range of other possible opportunities.

Gender

Gender was raised as a specific "at risk" factor by some countries. Australia noted that although girls stayed in school longer than boys there was little evidence that this extra experience widened their opportunities since they tended to choose areas of work and study with limited career potential. Few women went into business or industry and the skilled and semiskilled jobs were occupied mainly by men. In addition, the work was often part-time.

Germany noted that two-thirds of the applicants for vocational training were women and the majority were oriented towards a small spectrum of traditional female work that was also badly paid. They also had a higher risk of unemployment. It was also noted in Germany that boys benefited from a traditional aspect of family life whereby fathers and other menfolk supported them directly in finding work; a practice not available to girls presumably because of their perceived traditional roles. Although changes in life styles, smaller families and more freedom for both sexes were changing this pattern nevertheless, a family and community support existed more generally for boys than for girls.

Sex differences in outcomes were also noted in Sweden where there are trends for "at risk" boys to become aggressive and act as bullies in school, this being associated with alcoholism, drug abuse and criminality. Girls "at risk" were often shy and, being unaware of the implications of their developing sexuality, were frequently victims of sexually transmitted diseases and early and often unwanted pregnancy.

There are further implications of these issues which will be taken up in more detail in a later section of this report which considers issues relating to the transition to work for youth "at risk".

Prevalence

Estimating the true size of the "at risk" population is far from easy. Most OECD Member countries have no hard and fast definition and as a result statistics cannot readily be kept. However, having noted this point a number of countries have provided statistics which will now be reported within contexts identified by the countries concerned.

In Australia estimates were given of youth "at risk" aged between 15 and 19. In 1983, 20.3 per cent of this group were estimated to be "at risk". This figure had declined dramatically by 1989 to 11 per cent. These students showed a weakness in basic skills and usually failed to complete school. The report points out that average figures hide interesting differences by type of school, *i.e.* state, private or denominational and by district, urban or rural. (The urban/rural dimension had limited explanatory potential *per se* and required further breakdown.)

In Belgium statistics are not readily available. However studies have shown that 34 per cent of 5-year-olds were "at risk" of experiencing substantial difficulty in adapting to the first year of the primary school. Subsequently, 25 per cent had serious problems during the first year. After one year of primary school 30 per cent are "at risk". Turning to the school leavers, in 1984 it was estimated that 65 per cent of pupils left school with no qualifications. In Brussels it has been estimated that between 10 and 15 per cent of pupils left school early or were expelled while a different enquiry showed that 3 per cent of pupils following general and technical studies interrupted their courses during the first semester; the equivalent figure in the professional sector was 12 per cent.

In France, in the primary sector, 0.33 per cent of pupils attend initiation-adjustment classes.[1] In the secondary sector 2.2 per cent attend a variety of different types of classes. Thus taken together approximately 2.5 per cent are considered "at risk". However, considering the rather broader context of the Zones of Educational Priority it may be noted that approximately 15 per cent of pupils are seen to be in need of additional support.

In Germany, figures given relate only to those failing to gain qualifications and who for this reason are "at risk" of not obtaining employment. Six per cent leave school without certificates and 17.5 per cent drop out of vocational education.

In Italy, in 1986-87, 8.1 per cent dropped out of middle school and 24.7 per cent from the secondary superior school. In 1988-89, 11.7 per cent repeated the first year of middle school and 12 per cent the first year of secondary superior school.

In Japan, "at risk" children are viewed as those likely to be either school refusers or to drop out. School refusal in lower secondary schools has increased from 0.21 per cent in 1978 to 0.54 per cent in 1987. For those who drop out the numbers in 1987 increased in comparison with 1982 but the rate has decreased from 2.4 per cent in 1983 to 2.1 per cent in 1987. The level of juvenile delinquency peaked in 1983 at approximately 1.8 per cent but has been declining since. Solvent abuse shows different patterns for employed and unemployed youth. Since 1983 it has been declining for the employed youngsters but increasing at least up to 1987 for unemployed youth.

In the Netherlands, 47 per cent of primary aged children may be regarded as being "at risk". However, this figure drops to 5 per cent if only those who leave school without any form of certification are included. The figure of 47 per cent is derived from adding together the various groups who are used to calculate additional resource allocation. In the Netherlands, resources are weighted according to degree of "at risk" status according to a particular formula. The additional resources thus calculated are allocated to individual schools.

In Portugal, in 1987, the numbers of pupils who repeated a year was very high. For example 42.3 per cent repeated the second year. This dropped to 19.1 per cent in the 6th year although in the 7th and 8th year the figures rose again to 36 and 34 per cent respectively. About 10 per cent of pupils dropped out of school before the 6th year.

In the United Kingdom there is no straightforward definition of "at risk". Some 10 per cent of pupils have left school with no qualifications over recent years. Nationally an estimated 6 per cent of children truant, although the figure reaches 10 per cent in the cities. In addition there are a number of children of travellers (estimated at 12 000 to 15 000 in 1985) who probably receive little formal education.

In the United States, around 30 per cent of children under the age of 18 are considered to be "at risk" of educational failure. These estimates are based on 4 demographic factors of poverty, race and ethnic minority status, living in a one parent family and poor english proficiency. If, however, all of these factors are used to identify a population who are seriously "at risk", or even an underclass, then an estimate of between 6 an 8 per cent emerges. Although this represents a relatively small number of people in real terms the group tripled in size between 1970 and 1980.

To summarise – there is too much variability in definition to make a meaningful quantitative summary. Qualitatively, however, it is clear from the statistics described that CYAR present a substantial problem to many of the countries involved. (Additional figures, complementing those given here on school completion rates, etc., are available in *Education at a Glance*, OECD, 1995.)

National policies

The broad nature of the country based definitions of "at risk" given earlier imply that national policies need to be commensurately wide in scope if some headway is to be made with the problem. Thus any discussion of this topic which limited itself to education issues only would not do justice to the work received from the countries. However, it must be noted that a comprehensive consideration of national policies across administrative boundaries was well beyond the scope of the study and thus what follows reflects those areas of policy initiative where information was made available. It is assembled according to a range of widely used headings abstracted from the countries' descriptions.

It is a truism to say that OECD Member countries would like all of their children to make a sound start, to stay in school, not drop out and to make a smooth transition to work. However, many children do not follow this path, and policies have developed in all of these areas intended to help those "at risk". One of the central orientations is placing the child and not the system at centre stage or increasing system flexibility to meet child and family needs. Such an approach raises different issues in countries with, for instance, low population densities compared to those with high densities or in countries with central control of the curriculum compared to those with more localised control. These background considerations lead to the following identifiable areas of interest.

A sound start

OECD Member countries have policies which recognise that a sound start to life is required. This means healthy parents and babies. A preventive approach is recognised as a central feature and this necessitates the involvement of health and social welfare services and the provision of good housing as well as provision for adequate maternity leave. It is becoming more and more accepted that the child's cognitive and language development must also be stimulated during the preschool years and that the widespread provision of early childhood education can be extremely beneficial. This topic is discussed more fully in Chapter II.

School age

Policies and developments at this phase of education have the goal of increasing the flexibility of the system in order to engage the child and his/her family more fully in the educational process. Developments are taking place at a number of levels.

Structural/governance

Arrangements exist in all countries to make provision for pupils who are "at risk" and failing to make adequate progress. In many countries this often takes the form of separate provision in which education is provided, for instance, in custodial arrangements for young offenders (Italy) to help prevent recidivism, or in special schools for drop-outs (Japan). But in addition policies also exist for developing flexibility of provision within the existing school arrangements by increasing school autonomy. This may take the form, for instance, of freeing the school from an over constraining national curriculum, as in Italy, as well as encouraging schools to develop a wholistic management style (*e.g.* United States).

Although policies on school autonomy are aimed at giving those "at risk" greater access to the curriculum they have different manifestations. In Italy the idea is to develop co-operation between schools to provide a broad range of relevant provision. However, in the United Kingdom, the plan is to improve quality and raise standards by developing competition between schools based on market forces. These approaches can be conveniently divided into those that impact on school organisation, on curriculum and on pedagogy.

Organisational aspects

Various adaptations must be made in some countries in order to reach those children who live in isolated areas or who are mobile, and policies favouring the use of information technology and other distance learning methods have been formulated. Policies also are in place in order to lengthen teaching time and the school day. In the latter case this also includes the development of arrangements, *e.g.* in Japan, whereby the school day is extended for those who cannot attend during the day and is part of a lifelong learning policy. Policies for support both before and after the school day also exist in other countries such as Belgium and France for those children who would otherwise be without adult supervision. In some cases this extends beyond the preschool years.

Curriculum

At this level of the system, policies have been developed to make the curriculum more relevant and responsive to pupils' learning needs. Earlier noted policies to increase school autonomy allow schools more freedom to select curricula to fit local needs and either to by-pass centrally determined content, or to use different ways and means to achieve the centrally agreed objectives. Some countries have policies to allow for accelerated curriculum approaches for those "at risk" rather than using more traditional remedial methods.

Pedagogy

Policies also exist to help with support for mother tongue teaching for immigrants and also to allow schools to respond more sensitively to the pupils learning "rhythms" (France). In addition the development of information technology as a supportive teaching tool is being encouraged.

Links and transition to work

Over and above the issues so far identified, many countries have policies to encourage stronger links with the home, the community and business. In some countries, e.g. Ireland, parents constitutionally have a major role to play in their children's education and strengthening the links between home and school is viewed as a useful strategy for helping to overcome school failure. In Japan, links between schools and business are seen as helping drop-outs to gain relevant experience which helps in career decisions. In addition there is a possibility for the transfer of educational credits from business-based courses to schools. In many countries the value of a closer link between school and work is seen as valuable for those "at risk", for example in the dual system[2] in Germany. In the United Kingdom, policies are in place to encourage community initiatives via educational support grants which focus on inner city areas.

Resource targeting and policy co-ordination

It is self-evident that resources are limited and therefore targeting is crucial. It is clear from the discussion above on prevalence and definitional matters that many more children are estimated to be "at risk" than actually drop out or otherwise fail; an outcome which must be partly attributable to effective preventive policies and strategies. However, it is also likely that many of these children would have been false positives, i.e. would have been included under a broad "at risk" category but in reality were not educationally "at risk". For instance many children who come from single parent families may be perfectly well supported. This result points to the need for further refinements to be made to the definitions of "at risk" categories that may be used for instance in the calculation of additional resources to be provided.

Getting the allotted resources efficiently and effectively to those who are most in need has been tackled in some countries through the development of ZEPs (France) and

EPAs (Netherlands). In these areas special efforts are made to support locally identified initiatives and to improve awareness and practices of the professional staff involved; an approach which requires the co-ordination of policy.

This kind of approach may be contrasted with (the more expensive way?) of identifying individual children, as in the child-centred special educational needs model; a formal comparison that still needs to be made.

Other methods to improve the quality of services such as vouchers given to parents to encourage choice have also been on the policy agenda of some countries as a means of targeting resources.

Intervention strategies

In the previous section a description of national policies was outlined. National policies have a realisation in practice and in this section intervention strategies are considered from the point of view of age and stage. The section considers the periods of preschool, school and transition to work and this structure foreshadows the organisation of the later parts of the report.

Preschool

Although asked, countries responded in a very limited way on preschool issues, perhaps because in general preschool services lie outside the general concerns of Ministries of Education. Nevertheless, many countries either have, *e.g.* France, or are developing more comprehensive preschool services and recognise the need and importance of this phase in the overall development of the child.

The services that were described generally emphasised the importance of including the family, and the realisation of the significance of the family to preschool education appears to have grown. For instance in Australia services that were called preschool are now known as *early childhood family services centres* and are inter-disciplinary in function. Other countries noted schemes for the protection of abused children.

Three important terms emerged: *multi-disciplinarity, continuity* and the *role of education*. They are discussed further below.

Multi-disciplinarity

Countries recognise the importance of the co-ordination or integration of services in this area and the involvement of parents. This was perhaps described most fully in the United States report in the framework of the well known "headstart" project which provides support in income, health, nutrition, social services, housing and education for poor families.

Continuity

Several countries made it a point of concern that there should be continuity in provision for the pre-schooler. In Australia for instance it was particularly noted as being part of the development of the quality of relationship between teachers, parents and the child. The continuity of provision was also stressed by the United States, as children pass through preschool to kindergarten to elementary school programmes, in order to sustain gains.

Role of education

There is no great agreement on the part that formal educational experiences should play in preschool programmes. In France for instance it is very clear that preschools are *schools* and form the foundation of the French education system. Their objectives are to educate, socialise and teach children how to learn and practice. In contrast, a section in the United States report entitled "Characteristics of high quality offerings" does not mention the word "education". The discussion focuses on parental involvement, services integration, continuity of services, low numbers of children per care (Secretariat emphasis) giver and care givers having some early childhood training. While relevant educational experiences are perhaps implied in the section in the United States report on continuity, given that this emphasises the articulation between preschool and school, their goals could remain at the level of socialisation, with only informal attention given to literacy and numeracy skills. In such comparisons it is important to bear in mind the many dimensions and forms of early childhood education, which need not and often do not entail formal teaching of the basic skills of literacy and numeracy.

As noted, this section of the report is based on very limited information and it is unlikely that most of the participating countries who did not discuss preschool issues would find much difficulty in agreeing with the points made above. There is growing recognition that preschool work is important and that it has some kind of educational component. The general esteem with which the French *école maternelle* system is held by many countries suggests that the well developed explicit educational component is highly regarded; a view echoed in the French-American Foundation report following their visit to France (Richardson and Marx, 1989).

However, despite these positive statements the feeling remains that a great deal more could be done in OECD Member countries in this area to help children "at risk" receive more stimulating cognitive experiences and appropriate socialisation to help them benefit to the fullest extent possible later in schooling.

A full discussion of preschool issues appears in Chapter II of this report.

School age

It is clear from the country reports that there is no shortage of strategies that have been adopted in order to help overcome the learning problems of CYAR. They touched on almost all aspects of schooling and they must be interpreted as reflecting substantial dissatisfaction that the status quo is able to provide appropriate educational methods for

CYAR, who bring to school a heterogeneity of needs not previously recognised or catered for. For some countries they may even represent entirely new problems.

This view, however, does not extend to a wholesale rejection of the educational models in operation. Some countries did note a need for reform of fundamental education and curriculum change in secondary education. Experimental schools such as Magnet schools in the United States and CTCs (City Technology Colleges) in the United Kingdom have also been developed within this devolutionary approach. Such schools provide examples of curriculum change that is noted as needed by some countries. The United Kingdom has already embarked on major changes involving the development and implementation of a national curriculum which involves assessment of pupil progress in 10 curriculum subjects. There is an explicit intention to make certain aspects of school performance comparable and in this way to attempt to give parents a basis for informed choice. In certain States of the United States, there is a legal requirement for accountability of standards and States can intervene if necessary in the functioning of schools.

Other countries have not gone this far but the interest in effective schools and the whole school approach is strong and the changes that these movements imply, if implemented, would have fundamental implications for schools. A concern for the continuing effective education of CYAR is necessary if preschool gains are to be maintained, and if such a view is carried through then substantial implications follow in terms of method and organisation. One country noted that schools need to develop problem-solving approaches whereby, either individually or collectively they develop the means and strategies to analyse and respond to the learning difficulties presented by pupils.

Flexibility

School based approaches to developing flexibility have already been noted above. Some countries have chosen to implement policies intended to encourage adaptability through the development of priority areas set up to provide strategies to help decrease socio-economic, cultural and educational retardation. ZEPs in France have already been noted, but in addition there are Educational Priority Areas (EPAs) in the Netherlands and the Disadvantaged Schools Programmes (DSPs) in Australia.

Increased funding

Additional resources are often associated with such initiatives and can lead to real innovations. In the Netherlands, for instance, additional teaching staff are allocated by "weighting" pupils according to social and cultural background factors. From a baseline of 1.0, Dutch families from low socio-economic backgrounds attract a weighting of 1.25, Bargee's 1.4, Travellers 1.7 and ethnic minorities as 1.9. In the Netherlands, areas burdened by a cumulation of social, economic and cultural problems, receive extra resources for co-ordinating activities and for carrying out special projects. These areas comprise 10 to 20 schools and some welfare institutions working together in an area-based liaison. This is a similar idea to the ZEP in France although there additional funds can go to individual schools or groups depending on perceived needs. Both of these approaches have been the subject of evaluations with successful outcomes.

There are other approaches to getting funds through to disadvantaged areas such as educational support grants (ESGs) in the United Kingdom and "Chapter 1" of the American Government and the Disadvantaged Schools Programme in Australia. Evaluations of the DSP have reported success if medium to long-term perspectives are taken.

The Disadvantaged Schools Programme in Australia, set up in 1975, serves schools with concentrations of students from disadvantaged socio-economic circumstances. It helps them to develop programmes to benefit the education of the children by providing effective learning through more rewarding and relevant schooling and improved interaction between schools and communities. It emphasises whole school and community approaches and depends on joint participation of community groups, members of the school community and the education authorities.

In that country, allocation of funds to the individual state is determined by the number of disadvantaged students in it as identified by an index compiled from national census data. About 14 per cent of the national student population are covered. The DSP is administered by the relevant state education department in the government sector and the state catholic education commission in the non-government sector. Both establish administrative committees at state and regional levels and the commission involves non-government schools.

The committees, which must include parents and community members, review school objectives and draw up proposals for improving learning outcomes in schools. Funding allocated on the basis of need and the likely effectiveness of actual proposals rather than on a per capita basis, supports whole school change as follows:
- School based curriculum development to broaden life experiences and to increase self-confidence.
- To improve basic educational skills.
- To improve economic, political, organisational and technical knowledge for pupils to function effectively in society.
- To develop school/community liaison and participation of parents in the development and implementation of curriculum programmes.
- Programmes to involve pupils in expressive arts.
- Support to schools to allow them to document, evaluate and disseminate outcomes; this is co-ordinated and supported by systems at national level.

Evaluation is an integral part of this arrangement. A number of levels are involved. School committees:
- review school objectives;
- draw up proposals for improving learning outcomes, making curriculum more relevant, and create closer associations between parents and the community;
- develop evaluation programmes; and
- agree to a long term commitment (three years minimum) to ensure that programme goals are attained.

State systems are accountable to the Federal Government for the educational context, the use of money, for participation and retention and developing the capacity of the teaching force.

Outcomes of these programmes have revealed that fundamental skills have increased, especially in basic educational attainments. There have been improved attitudes to school and increased enthusiasm and improved student attendance and a decrease in discipline problems. There has also been an increase in parent and community involvement.

Teachers have also proved more responsive to community needs and have developed a better knowledge of planning, continuity and sequence. They can also better relate their activities to programme objectives. All in all the programme is a stimulus to better practice. It appears to work and funds get through to the disadvantaged.

School level interventions

The intervention strategies that have been described by OECD Member countries are wide ranging, clearly recognising that for schools to be effective in educating *all* children substantial reform is necessary and must take into account the child in his or her broader social and domestic context. Furthermore, strategies and resources must be available in order to compensate for those aspects of living which perforce need to be fulfilled and for effective education to be possible. Important themes that underlie the issues identified by the countries include measures to:

- extend time available for learning, to ensure continuity across phases of learning, *e.g.* preschool to school, school to work;
- make the curriculum relevant;
- develop individual pedagogy and introduce change into classroom arrangements and teacher pupil interactions;
- support the child's personal social/emotional needs;
- use a range of external services; and
- increase freedom to schools and teachers.

These themes are elaborated below.

Increase in time

A key theme which drives improved learning is merely significantly increasing the effective time spent learning; many of the strategies identified are intended to achieve the goal of increasing time on task. At the most fundamental level, OECD Member countries discussed the extension of the compulsory period of education or the introduction of means to assist CYAR to stay on at school after the compulsory age had been passed. Some countries have extended this age to 18 (*e.g.* Belgium) while for others it stops at 14 (*e.g.* Italy).

The success of such an extension for CYAR appears to be mixed and effectiveness depends on style and organisation. Little detail was given in the reports. Sweden, however, pointed out that for some CYAR the increased flexibility of upper secondary school was beneficial and difficulties experienced by certain children in secondary school disappeared in upper secondary. Nevertheless, the report also indicated that school management needed to provide support to some teachers who could be insensitive to the needs of CYAR.

Lengthening of the school day was also seen as a way to provide additional time on task and in the United States, work with "Comer" schools which try to provide accelerated learning have experimented successfully with this approach.

In Japan, flexibility of use of school resources in their "special training" and "miscellaneous" schools are seen as a way of coping with diversification of the careers of young people as well as a means of reducing drop-out. These schools offer a wide variety of practical, vocational and technical educational programmes to meet new diverse needs. They can offer very flexible attendance patterns such as the possibility of early morning or late evening enrolment. In addition they offer second chance learning as well as additional courses for those studying in higher education. They are a central pivot of Japan's lifelong learning strategy. In addition the schools may qualify pupils for university entrance.

Increasing learning time in regular schools has been addressed through programmes which provide supervised homework services and educationally relevant extra-curricula activities.

At the furthest extreme countries have found it necessary to provide alternative educational settings to meet the needs of youth who have experienced extensive school failure and who have little or no family support. These children are not having their basic needs met and may become involved in substance abuse. Success in such schools depends on inter-agency collaboration and community involvement, changed curricula and so on. In more extreme cases, still other countries (e.g. Italy) have developed educational inputs in custodial settings.

Curriculum

As noted in the previous section, curriculum change has frequently been identified as essential for educational programmes to be successful with CYAR. Many countries pointed to needed reform in this area content, method, programmes and assessment procedures. It is essential to take into account the needs of ethnic minorities via, for example, an inter-cultural approach. This allows for some teaching in the minority language as well as the opportunity for the various cultures to learn about each other's assumptions, values and approaches and to give them a status equivalent to that of the principal culture.

While many countries emphasised the importance of developing basic educational attainments (and success in this domain formed the core of many intensive efforts), other approaches for older children included the development of projects both in the school and the wider community involving media and business enterprise projects.

Pedagogical factors

Almost all countries pointed to the need for substantial development to take place in the classroom experiences of the child. These are discussed under the headings of classroom arrangements and teacher-pupil interactions.

- *Classroom arrangements*

It was widely recognised that successful teaching of CYAR depended on adopting an approach which was preventive/diagnostic in nature, which gave the opportunity for intensive remediation and individualisation, emphasising the importance of adapting working styles to the needs of the child. Mixed age and mixed ability approaches to classroom organisation were seen as being appropriate as were methods of team teaching, providing generally lower teacher-pupil ratios that could be achieved, for example through intensive remedial work either outside the main class (pull-out programmes) or within it. Flexibility was seen as a key organising construct which could be encouraged through peer tutoring, the use of trainee teachers and other means.

- *Teacher-pupil interactions*

Three sub-components emerged with the goal of individualisation in mind. First, countries reported a need to improve the personal-emotional links between teacher and pupils and to improve communication. Second, more sensitivity needed to be shown to immigrants with a requirement to develop inter-cultural pedagogy. Third, the pupils themselves should be given a greater role. This point was made especially forcefully in the Australian report. At the classroom level, students are seen as having an important role to play in decision-making about the curriculum, assessment through negotiation and, as noted above, involvement through projects within and out of the school. Pupils can also gain much value through peer tutoring.

Children's personal and social needs

Many countries pointed to the importance of attending to the pupils' affective needs throughout the duration of school time. It was seen as important that pupils were secure from harassment and discrimination, healthy, emotionally stable and socially well adjusted. This idea is well encapsulated through an approach identified as a "student management/discipline code" as described in the Australian report.

External involvement and links

Maintaining effective cognitive and emotional development of pupils was seen as involving the establishment of links with external agencies across the age span. They fall into a number of categories – this section will pick up some of the themes identified earlier. All countries emphasised the importance of parental involvement and see home-school liaison as critical to successful educational progress. In Ireland, parents are seen as the principal educators of their children with those "at risk" being largely in that position because of a breakdown between the home and the school. Involving parents in schools is therefore crucial. Parental involvement is also viewed as important from the point of view of school governance with many countries having parents on school boards. In addition, *e.g.* in the United Kingdom and United States, parental involvement is seen as a way of developing accountability for schools and improving standards.

Parents are also naturally regarded as a link with the community and again many countries viewed community involvement as equally crucial. Community involvement took several forms but the inclusion of business was taken to be important for the maintenance of continuity and the development of careers and for career advice.

Links with business were also identified as important in the development of the enterprise spirit, which is being fostered across a wide age spread, in Australia for example.

Several countries noted the importance of strengthening the link between services such as school psychologists and other guidance teams (*e.g.* psycho-pedagogues) as well as other services. These have been noted before but are worth repeating; they include housing, health, family assistance and support outside of school hours. In addition changes to teacher training and in-service education of teachers (INSET) to help teachers to become more sensitive to the needs of "at risk" pupils were also endorsed.

In the United Kingdom, educational support grants (ESGs) have been used to support youth programmes in inner city areas as well as "drop-in" learning centres. Community education has of course a long history in the United Kingdom. It emphasises home-school links and opens up the school to community use in out-of-school hours. In addition the curriculum in these schools would reflect local conditions. While considerable success has been claimed for this approach, formal evaluations have not been carried out.

Increased freedom to schools and teachers

Certain countries, especially those with centrally controlled curricula (*e.g.* Italy), raised the issue of developing effective ways for teachers and schools to have the adequate freedom to modify teaching methods and for curricula content to meet the needs present in local conditions.

Summary

The intervention strategies identified in the country reports and noted above make an obviously challenging agenda. If reform is needed to the extent that is implied, it is not surprising that most schools have been unable to develop approaches which work effectively with those pupils who under the current arrangements have no realistic chance of success. Schools, of course, take the blame because it is their job to educate all children, but the range of intervention strategies identified above reveal that in reality the problem in need of solution extends much further into the core of the functioning of societies.

The emerging answer to these difficulties is cast in terms of the effective school literature and in particular the whole school approach. This has been articulated most fully in the Australian report where the approach to educational reform reflects, in a co-ordinated way, the perceived needs of the 21st century. The reforms treat education as a major instrument for achieving social justice for all through changes in the way schools function including curriculum, school organisation, links with external services and pedagogic style. The Australian report gives an idea of the scope of the task where school systems must weave the following strands of strategy into a seamless garment. There are five federal programmes covering:

    i) poverty and disadvantage;
    ii) geographic isolation;
    iii) ethnicity and English as a second language;
    iv) aboriginality; and
    v) gender.

Complementary State and Territory initiatives to develop a student-management discipline code involve:

- student participation;
- student enterprise;
- peer tutoring;
- pastoral care;
- self-protective behaviours (*e.g.* versus abuse);
- literacy and numeracy skills;
- parental participation;
- school industry links;
- labour market awareness;
- post-compulsory education (organisational structures, curriculum initiatives);
- school, technical college and further educational co-operation;
- alternative settings; and
- school linked accommodation programmes.

Effective schools link the issues together in a whole school approach "which integrates all groups in the school, students, staff, parents and community and recognises and values each group in the process of participation, negotiation, decision-making and co-operation".

Chapter III looks in more detail at ways in which schools can change.

Transition to work

It is clear from the reports that the problem of transition to work for those "at risk" is taken very seriously in OECD Member countries. It is an area in which there has been an abundance of change and development of approaches across a wide spectrum of possibilities. The problem is taken to be important simply because a large proportion of CYAR fail to get work and even in countries where unemployment has fallen recently there are instances (*e.g.* the Netherlands) where it has risen in ethnic minorities and youth. Women too experience particular difficulty and in Germany, the Netherlands and

Sweden the point is made that gains made at school are lost in the transition to work and job securing period.

The reforms and developments discussed below recognise sometimes explicitly (*e.g.* Sweden) that in the 1970s and 1980s, school goals and work needs had become unhitched and are in need of recoupling. It is recognised that if this remarriage is to be made on earth (and even in heaven!) that the substantial realignments in many areas of education, business and support structures, already initiated, should be continued.

The analysis which underlies the changes emphasises a number of key points. Pupils have either inadequate or wrong skills, and inappropriate attitudes to work and their role in a hierarchy. The following discussion identifies and discusses critical solutions, at a wide range of levels of the system, to counteracting these flaws.

Development of useful skills

School-industry links

Links between schools and industry/business are a strong feature of the approach taken in many countries to develop relevant skills. This is a way of bringing schools around to their demands and thus making curriculum adjustments to deacademicise their approach (*e.g.* Italy) as well as giving pupils the opportunity to see the possibilities on offer and to motivate them to develop relevant skills and labour market awareness (Australia, Italy). For Sweden there is hope that work-place experiences will improve school work quality. However, evaluations have not supported this expectation. In France, too, these links are intended to improve the match between employers' and trainees' expectations and aspirations.

A variety of approaches have been adopted. In Australia, school industry links have involved employers, trade unions, teachers, parents and students in developing responses aimed to link school and local business, promote study, develop teachers' awareness and to get business and trades unions to understand schooling more fully.

In the United Kingdom "compacts" have been developed between school and industry along the lines of the Boston compacts whereby employers find work for students who reach agreed standards. It may be noted that 67 per cent of 15 year olds (in 1986) got work placements. In the United Kingdom, schemes such as the Technical Vocational Educational Initiative (TVEI) and Youth Training Scheme (now Youth Training) have also been developed to give school curriculum a more job oriented aspect. School/business links have a strong tradition in Belgium where regular contacts between education, business and the community take place in areas of high unemployment. Technical and professional schools in the main co-operate in this arrangement. Since the extension of the compulsory education period to 18 years of age, more pupils spend some time in businesses.

In France, the responsibility of developing the transition to work phase has recently become a mission of the education system. This includes working with drop-outs who

have re-established contact with schools. It has been recognised that continuity in the life stages are important and that transition to work is as important a stage as entering school. This youth integration strategy (*Le dispositif d'insertion des jeunes de l'éducation natio-nale – DIJEN*) is based on three principles:

  i) Guidance and monitoring of young people
  This includes an individual assessment of skills, abilities and motivation.

  ii) Work study programmes
  This includes alternating study with on the job experience. It requires real dialogue between companies and teachers to ensure coherence between work experience and training programmes. Placements must be satisfying and help to overcome feelings of failure. The relationship between pupil and teacher is crucial.

  iii) Individualisation
  This is the establishment of a plan with each pupil that corresponds with his/her aspirations and on an acceptable timescale. This approach, which runs against the traditional structures of the National Educational System involves busi-nesses. It can also develop increased opportunities for "training credit facili-ties" and a new formula for "personalised schemes for gaining qualifications". This is especially important for those who wish to return to school during the course of the year.

In Sweden SYO (study and vocational guidance) was set up to counteract the academicisation of school and to bridge school and work. It is also intended to counteract restriction in vocational choice. Pupils are required to have 6-10 weeks work experience with equal opportunity emphasis. In the upper secondary, SYO is similar in objectives and organisation, although work experience is longer.

Post-secondary

Similar developments can be identified in the post-secondary sector although in this phase links with business and the opportunity of apprenticeship have a much longer history. In Germany, in 1989, 72 per cent of youth between the ages of 18 and 25 were either in the "dual system" or had passed through it.

This close relationship still left 13 per cent of eligible young people (approximately two-thirds being girls) without a vocational training. The remaining 15 per cent use other routes such as universities. Given that minority groups are over-represented in the lower echelons of German education, it is likely that those "at risk", because of ethnic minority status or socio-economic disadvantage, constitute a large proportion of this 13 per cent and will have an increased risk of unemployment. Furthermore, German businesses are unprepared to take responsibility for all pupils during times of financial crisis.

However, not all school leavers gain a contract in vocational training. Six per cent leave school with no final certificate and only 2.4 per cent of those become apprentices. Thus the majority of this group of school leavers does not gain a recognised vocational education. Seventeen point five per cent of all contracts fail, the rate being especially high for vocations such as hairdresser (38 per cent) and painter and varnisher (35 per cent), in contrast to bank clerk (2.5 per cent). Finally for those who do not have the appropriate entry level qualifications for the vocational education programmes, prevocational education programmes have been set up.

Other countries too have responses which, though less well developed follow the same lines. In France, for instance, among other things the GRETA (*Groupement d'établissements pour la formation des adultes*) scheme (a decentralised and co-ordinated network for adult training), has facilitated the setting up of "on-the-job" training schemes for young people that are directly related to local situations and which are cognisant of business needs. It aims to improve the match between those offering placements and the trainees themselves – one of the leitmotivs is the individualisation of the training schemes.

A variety of post-compulsory schemes are offered in the United States, where low achieving students are obliged to take more vocational education. Interestingly, studies have shown that courses taken may not be the best planned and may serve to narrow unnecessarily the choice of programmes. Students are less likely to have the opportunity to try out jobs and less able to attend courses giving in-depth instruction. This downward spiral of those with less initial opportunity receiving degraded experiences, thus narrowing choice even further, is a phenomenon that the Swedish SYO plan was partly intended to help overcome.

Schemes in the United States, provided for example under the Job Training Partnership Act (JTPA), offer comprehensive programmes which balance job training with summer work and academic remediation. A particularly successful example has been the Jobcorps which is a residential (5 months) programme for "out-of-school" disabled youth. Evaluations have shown that those attending such courses were employed longer, earned more, were more likely to get diplomas and suffered fewer arrests.

More recent developments involve close collaboration between post-secondary institutions and employers to provide training for employees and potential employees in "customised training".

In Japan "miscellaneous" and "special training" schools have been developed that offer flexible opening times for students before and after work. In addition, they offer alternative approaches to "drop-outs" as well as other students. These schools also have links with business, as already noted, and the possibility of accreditation transfer exists between business and schools. Furthermore, some special training colleges can offer a path of entry to universities.

In Australia, changes in post-secondary education have emphasised co-operative programmes between schools and university campuses and have developed senior and junior structures to give pupils continuity of experience when changing from one structure to another. Tertiary colleges also offer flexible attendance times and have *crèches*. In addition, open access colleges have been set up.

There have also been curriculum initiatives such as a certificate of vocational training. Increasing flexibility and pathways to higher education are also goals. Counselling is also provided and there is a general effort to give technical and applied knowledge more value in the curriculum.

Community provision

Initiatives have also been taken to provide additional community based services. In the United Kingdom, under the auspices of the Educational Support Grant, a scheme is in place to develop the role of youth workers in inner cities in order to encourage alternative routes to qualifications for those who might find access to such courses through conventional means difficult. In addition, open learning or ''drop-in'' centres have been established to help adults in need develop literacy and other skills. In Australia, Youth Access Centres (YACs) have also been introduced to serve similar purposes.

Multi-agency approaches

For some countries it has become clear that the period of transition to work requires the co-ordinated involvement of a number of agencies. These provide examples of interesting and contrasting service rules, an issue which is taken up more fully in the next section on cross-cutting issues. In the Netherlands, an improved system helping those ''at risk'' to find jobs is being stimulated via new policies to link ministries. These plan to:

- co-ordinate policies for adult education;
- collaborate with trades unions and employers to use existing programmes and infrastructures more fully; and
- combine separate budgets controlled by different ministries.

In Australia, co-operation between schools, universities, research organisations, trades unions and businesses is planned as part of a general strategy to broaden post-school options, promote labour market awareness and facilitate learning for all involved about the realities of each other's current experiences.

In addition, regional multi-agency approaches bring together nutritional support, appropriate pedagogy and in-school services, such as counselling and medical support, within school programmes.

Health and welfare needs are also co-ordinated across the States and Territories. For instance, the Child and Adolescent Mental Health Services (CAMHS) are administered from two major hospitals in South Australia and provides a flexible array of services both within and out of the hospital.

In Germany, policies to co-ordinate activities of welfare agencies, businesses, schools and employment and training companies have been set up to help with the transition in former eastern *Länder*, from the centrally planned to the market economy.

In Portugal also there is extensive development of multi-agency community actions intended to improve organisation and encourage social integration of minorities and job finding. In addition, the importance of access to leisure and cultural activities is recognised, supported and involves parents.

Summary

It is clear that substantial efforts have been taken by OECD Member countries to help children and youth "at risk" make a successful transition from school to work. Many of the examples given show the need for multi-agency action and the co-ordination of government policies. Furthermore, in the United States, various forms of tax incentive have been offered to companies to help them absorb those "at risk" – although it must be mentioned that the take up of this incentive has not been strong – and financial support given to students in order to help them during this period. Many of the keywords that come from these findings reflect such concepts as flexibility of offerings, continuity of experiences, individualisation of method of support, multi-agency support, hands-on experience, school/business/community links and curriculum change. All of these are intended to better fit "the man to the job" and "the job to the man". It is clear that in spite of all of this effort there is still substantial progress to be made not only on the co-ordination front but also in establishing course content. In the United States, there is disagreement over whether course content should be general or specific in nature.

There is perhaps some ray of hope in the Australian work where a comprehensive attack in this area is described. It is interesting to note that the proportion of children "at risk" has declined substantially. In the older age groups (15-19 years) between 1986 and 1989 from 14.3 to 11.0 per cent.

The United States report also emphasises a comprehensive approach and sums up the qualities of effective drop-out programmes as:
- having smaller teaching groups to increase self-esteem and motivation;
- hands-on learning opportunities;
- focusing on formal instruction as well as family socio-economic conditions that effect likelihood of success at school; and
- emphasising career preparation.

Additional study time could also be added.

These points have been reflected in many of the contributions reviewed. The case studies are discussed fully in Chapter IV.

Cross-cutting issues

Countries were asked to comment on cross-cutting issues – aspects of the arrangements which impact horizontally or vertically on the system of support for CYAR. Almost all countries identified a need for increased co-operation between agencies, although it appears to have developed further in some countries than others. The following discussion brings together points made at different levels of the system.

Inter-sectoral co-operation

Effective in-roads into social and educational difficulties faced by those "at risk" require co-operation between various agencies. Portugal, for example, has set up an inter-ministerial programme (PIPSE) which is a unified approach operating at central, local and school levels. The programme is co-ordinated by a central or co-ordinating council and involves representation of the Ministry of Education, the Ministry of Planning and Administration of the Territory, the Ministry of Agriculture Fisheries and Food, the Ministry of Health, the Ministry of Employment and Social Security and the Ministry of Youth.

The programme is intended mainly to reduce failure in school by giving priority to the first levels of basic education (cycle 1) and to the most under-privileged socio-cultural environments where drop-out and grade repetition are especially frequent. The programme is comprehensive in coverage and it works collaboratively with health and nutritional services, support for families, development of a transport system and the organisation of leisure and sport activities in addition to pedagogical reform including additional assistance with equipment.

Beneath the co-ordinating council a management commission reflecting the structure of the council is responsible for local implementation. Local needs are identified by the President of the Council and a primary school teacher who maintains close collaboration with the Management Commission. They co-ordinate activities at the municipal level, ensure funding and run the Activity Teams. Activity Teams are also multi-disciplinary and ensure the effective implementation of the programme and its resources.

There is strong inter-sectoral collaboration in other countries also. In Australia, commonly agreed national goals for schooling are used as a basis for collaboration and co-operation between schools, States and Territories and the Federal government. Although it has not proved easy to define common curricula across schools, in certain cases, attempts have been made to ensure that local goals are commensurate with national goals. States and Territories provide funding and Federal government identifies National Priorities in consultation. This tier of government, as already noted, also funds particular programmes such as the Disadvantaged Schools Programme and requires financial and educational accountability, gender equality and special evaluation with regard to the particular programmes.

Other OECD Member countries report varying degrees of co-operation such as integrating training systems involving co-operation between the public education system and other Ministries, as well as recognising the importance of the family, local authorities and youth associations (Catholic and nondenominational), in Italy and in fighting AIDS in Greece.

Inter-sectoral co-operation and collaboration is also described in countries where particular measures have been taken to meet the needs of the disadvantaged. In the Netherlands, as mentioned above, Educational Priority Areas (EPAs) have been established to institute special facilities and resources. However, the boundaries of responsibility are reported to be unclear between education and other sectors. For example, early childhood programmes are mostly run by the Ministry of Welfare, Health and Cultural

Affairs. But reception projects for early school leavers involve education and science, social affairs, employment and justice ministries. Co-ordination, consistency and continuity are reported as lacking. Belgium also reports difficulties in working between sectors.

In Ireland home school community liaison projects bring together the activities of voluntary and statutory services co-ordinated by teachers. The aim of this approach is to de-emphasise the school as the sole agent in the education process and to re-enforce the role of the parent as the primary educator of the child – a point recognised in the Irish constitution.

The plan is that this action will develop a concept of community-based education, empower parents, develop a co-operative responsibility for children's education between parents and teachers, a more positive attitude to school and ameliorate behaviour and discipline problems. Seven clusters of schools have been identified (4 to 13 schools per cluster).

There is a national co-ordinator (a primary school head-teacher) whose job it is to animate local co-ordination and correspond with the National Steering Committee (NSC).

The NSC is chaired by a representative of the Ministry of Education and includes other groups interested in education including research (educational, economic and social), teachers, parents, religious and community leaders and the police.

The project is to be evaluated by looking at figures relating to truancy/attendance, vandalism, home profiles (housing, crime rates, employment status) involvement of parents in school and education, use of public libraries. So far the initiative has been well received by teachers and parents.

The need to integrate various forms of support to improve the social and educational opportunities for the disadvantaged has also been recognised in France. The first cycle of ZEP involved selecting priority areas to receive additional resources in the form of teachers and operational subsidies via the Ministry of Education. However, many of these areas were also receiving priority assistance for urban renewal and social support through the DSQ (*Développement social des quartiers*), a programme administered by the Ministry of the Cities. In 1990 these two initiatives were merged to strengthen the ZEP programme. This new policy involves a comprehensive city development policy including town planning, geographical and social environment, and cultural and social development for disadvantaged areas.

This convergence revealed the need for partnerships between schools and local authorities (municipalities, departments, general councils, regional councils) and the need to establish strong links between statutory services (health and social affairs) within an education policy concerned to solve social problems.

Extending schools' capabilities of responding effectively to the needs of disadvantaged pupils considered in the local context has led many countries to review the balance of control that exists between central and local demands. As pointed out in the Netherlands' report this immediately raises the question of who is responsible for maintenance of quality. This is a complex issue and here is not the place to develop the arguments in detail. Many countries see the solution as lying in locally controlled development (at the school or municipality level as described earlier in this chapter) but with some form of accountability to central government as the main funding agency. One particular issue raised frequently by countries related to the control of additional resources frequently given through formula funding for disadvantaged groups. Some countries (*e.g.* the Netherlands, Sweden and the United Kingdom) provide additional funds to schools on this basis but they are not earmarked and it remains unclear how they are used and which use is most effective. In the Netherlands, additional funds have often been used to decrease pupil-teacher ratios – an approach which is as likely to benefit the advantaged as it is the disadvantaged. Increasing the accountability of the use of these funds as in the United States and developing awareness of the need for introducing approaches that positively discriminate is an objective now of Dutch EPAs. Cost-effectiveness analyses are needed to help find the best way forward.

The implications of these approaches and their impact on the type and method of educational innovation and reform is worthy of further study. For instance, in the United States there is heavy dependence on evaluation methods to justify the use of funds. If such methods emphasise traditional cause-effect models of human development (as they tend to do) then this methodology will itself strongly influence the nature of the educational reform. This may or may not be good. But the implications are not widely analysed or well understood.

In addition, increasing the involvement of parents in schools is also a generally identifiable trend. The situation in Ireland has already been described. Parent involvement in decision-making is being encouraged in France and Sweden and is well advanced in other countries such as Belgium and the United Kingdom. In addition some countries have given parents more or less a free choice in their selection of school (*e.g.* Belgium and the Netherlands) while others are developing this approach (*e.g.* the United Kingdom).

Evolving new governance arrangements and empowering parents is a high priority for developing schools, as is implementing an appropriate management strategy. However, for schools to effectively meet the challenges of greater inclusion and the raising of standards for all pupils, internal school changes also need to occur.

Well articulated plans to encourage such an approach have been described by Australia. For that country, effective schools (*i.e.* those working within Australia's social justice objectives for all to create a skilled and educated community) adopt a whole school approach. This is supported by:
- strong teacher training;
- development of a democratic partnership between staff, students, parents and community;
- comprehensive student service networks, *e.g.* counsellors, parents and community and education workers, social workers, guidance officers, school nurses, attendance officers and in some States police liaison officers;
- links between community and government agencies; and
- review processes at State/Territory level leading to the development of policies and programmes for improved schooling.

From this approach a culture of co-operation is emerging, for instance in the multi-agency approach which is aimed to provide a system of educational training that is responsive to the needs of youth and of the region. The issue of agencies working effectively together was raised by many countries as in need of attention in order to harmonise policies to increase the effectiveness of services and to avoid overlap between them.

However, it must be noted that developing co-ordinated services is not a straight-forward process since it involves substantial change in the way systems currently operate. Because of the importance of this approach, exactly how co-operation has developed and can be encouraged would be worthy of further study.

Concluding comment

This chapter has brought together a large amount of information contained in the country reports. Taken as a whole, it points to the need for substantial change to be introduced if the education and other services involved are to make an appropriate response to CYAR. No general view emerged suggesting that this challenge requires a dismantling of the present system, but rather that developments are required to make it more responsive to the needs of children, their families and the communities in which they live and work.

The key points to emerge are described below.

Keypoints

Definition of children and youth "at risk"

Children and youth "at risk" are those pupils from disadvantaged backgrounds who fail to reach the necessary standards in school, often drop-out and as a consequence fail to become integrated into a normally accepted pattern of social responsibility, particularly with regard to work and adult life. There are many manifestations of a failure to integrate successfully, such as health problems, substance and drug abuse, crime, early pregnancy and unemployment.

Why the concern?

Demographic changes mean that fewer young people will be available to support increasingly ageing populations. Technological changes mean that those young people will have to be significantly better skilled. Countries which succeed in equipping disad-vantaged youth with high level skills and positive work attitudes are more likely to maintain economic prosperity and social cohesion and at the same time help to improve social justice and equity.

The concept of "at risk" is an optimistic one and emphasises prevention

The concept of "at risk" is an optimistic one if it moves the debate forward by recognising the transactional nature of much learning. In the educational context this means that the right educational experiences over time can help to compensate for disadvantage and optimise the chances of success for all pupils. A major advantage of the term is that it emphasises prevention in contrast to remedial approaches to the problem.

Factors associated with "at risk" status

A number of factors have been identified that are associated with failure in school, some of which have been used in research studies to identify "at risk" students. The general factors are:
- poverty;
- ethnic minority status;
- aspects of family arrangements (*e.g.* single parent status, level of education, housing adequacy, home-school breakdown, child abuse);
- poor knowledge of the majority language;
- type of school;
- the geographical location of the school; and
- community factors such as poor housing.

"At risk" factors are cumulative. One factor is associated with school failure with the same probability as no factors. But four factors is associated with a 10-fold increase in negative outcome.

Prevalence

Estimates of the prevalence of children and youth "at risk" vary substantially between OECD Member countries. Figures between 15 and 30 per cent are frequently quoted.

National policies

A wide range of national policies have been developed to tackle the problems presented by those "at risk". They emphasise placing the child at the centre of the system, individualising teaching approaches as well as those of other support services, and developing flexibility in provision to meet child and family needs.

This approach has implications for change across the system as a whole, for instance in the way schools are governed and organised, for curriculum and pedagogy. The way resources are targeted (*e.g.* directly to schools or areas where there is particular need) and policies co-ordinated is also a vital consideration.

Intervention strategies

A large number of intervention strategies have been developed, including co-ordinating services, concern for continuity across transition periods, flexibility in approach, greater autonomy for schools, changes in school organisation, developments in curriculum and pedagogy, closer attention to children's personal and social needs, and greater freedom for teachers especially regarding time to develop the best teaching strategies and resources and links with community businesses.

Evaluation

The evaluation of intervention strategies is a key issue for effective implementation and for stimulating change.

Inter-sectoral co-operation

Inter-sectoral co-operation is generally agreed to be essential to achieving effective policies and programmes for improved schooling. This involves collaboration between government departments and other agencies. The development of teacher training, pre-service and in-service, is a crucial factor. Effective links between the home, school, the community and other services are also key areas for co-operation.

Notes

1. These are classes which help pupils to orient to the demands of French schools.
2. The dual system is a co-operation of private companies and state schools controlled by Federal law. Private companies offer apprenticeships and apprentices must spend 1-2 days each week in school.

References

BARATZ, S.S. and BARATZ, J.C. (1970), "Early childhood intervention: the social science basis of institutionalised racism", *Harvard Educational Review*, Vol. 40, pp. 29-50.

BERNSTEIN, B. (1975), *Class, Codes and Control*, Routledge and Kegan Paul, London.

BOURDIEU, P. (1984), *Distinction, a Social Critique of the Judgement of Taste*, HUP Publications, London.

FREEDBERG, L. (1987), "The risks of labelling kids at risk", Baltimore Sun, Baltimore.

GERRY, M. (1992), "Economic consequences", in McLaughlin, M.J. Florian, L. Neubert, D. Boyd-Kjellen, G. and Frieden, L. (eds), *Transitions to Employment: Proceedings of the 1990 International Symposium of Persons with Disabilities*, University of Maryland at College Park.

HAVIGHURST, R.J. (1965), "Who are the socially disadvantaged?", *Journal of Negro Education*, Vol. 40, pp. 210-217.

KOHN, M.L. and SCHOOLER, C. (1985), *Work and Personality*, Homewood.

LEVIN, H. (1986), "The educationally disadvantaged are still among us", unpublished manuscript, Stanford University School of Education, Stanford, CA.

NATRIELLO, G., MCDILL, E.L. and PALLAS, A.M. (1990), *Schooling Disadvantaged Children: Racing Against Catastrophe*, Teachers College Press, New York.

OECD (1991), *Education and Cultural and Linguistic Pluralism*, CERI/CD(91)15, free document, Paris.

OECD (1993), *Access to Education and Training, Participation and Equity*, DEELSA/ED(93)8, free document, Paris.

OECD (1995), *Education at a Glance – OECD Indicators*, Paris.

PASSOW, A.H. (1970), "Deprivation and disadvantage: nature and manifestations", in Passow, A.H. (ed), *Deprivation and Disadvantage: Nature and Manifestations*, International Studies in Education, 21, pp. 15-51, Unesco Institute of Education, Hamburg, Germany.

RICHARDSON, G., and MARX, E. (1989), *A Welcome For Every Child*, French-American Foundation, New York.

RUTTER, M. (1980), *Changing Youth in a Changing Society: Patterns of Adolescent Development and Disorder*, Harvard University Press, Cambridge, Massachussetts.

RUTTER, M., and MADGE, N. (1976), *Cycles of Disadvantage*, Heinmann, London.

SCHORR, L.B. (1988), *Within Our Reach: Breaking the Cycle of Disadvantage*, Anchor Press/Doubleday, New York.

SIMON, B. (1971), *Intelligence, Psychology and Education*, Lawrence and Wishart, London.

STODOLSKY, S., and LESSER, J. (1967), "Learning patterns in the disadvantaged", *Harvard Educational Review*, 37, pp. 546-593.

Chapter II

Programmes and Issues Related to Early Childhood

by

Josette Combes
Association des Collectifs Enfants/Parents/Professionnels, Paris

Introduction

This chapter focuses on issues of prevention for preschool children "at risk". All children attend school, and school is the first place where their degree of adjustment to the society in which they live is measured. Prior to this period of "compulsory" socialisation, the family is expected to be responsible for the psychological, social and cognitive development of children as well as their physiological and emotional welfare.

However, changing life-styles and, in particular, the growing number of working mothers, coupled with important discoveries about how early children develop skills, have radically transformed the approach to this period in a person's life, and consequently the concept of prevention has also undergone considerable change. Today, professionals and experts feel that programmes to counter exclusion, underachievement and marginalisation must include preventive action directed to children from birth to age six.

Nonetheless, this recent trend of thought is by no means paralleled by practice and, even though there is no longer any argument about the value of a preschool approach, it is in this area that the inequalities are still the most flagrant.

This chapter prefaces a description of the programmes that have been examined during the course of this study with a general analysis of the various phenomena that affect a young child's life. The concepts of risk and "prevention" will be analysed from the specific standpoint of the preschool-age child.

The major developments that have direct repercussions on young children's lives

Demographic

All the countries covered in this study have, to a varying degree, experienced a decline in the number of births, with the birth rate in most of them now averaging less than two children per family. This dramatic drop in fertility, made possible by the wider availability of contraception methods, is to some extent offset by an equally substantial drop in infant mortality. These trends have resulted in a different attitude towards children – births tend to be planned. The child's position within the family has become less peripheral and part of a scheme wherein the various aspects – timing, space and the nature of the emotional and material investment – have been taken into consideration.

However, this broad trend does not apply to those families who do not possess the necessary means of managing their existence due to a lack of information, insufficient control over their own lives, lack of intellectual and material resources, different beliefs and customs, etc. In such cases, families have more difficulties in providing their children with the environment, care and intellectual support that are common in other families, so that they start with a disadvantage vis-à-vis the average child.

Socio-economic

In many young households both parents work. The entry of women into the labour market is a phenomenon which was accelerated by the industrial revolution, gathered momentum as the result of two world wars and became an accepted aspect of women's fight for equal rights. One of the premises of feminist movements, and one which is virtually irrefutable in the context of equal rights, is the importance of economic independence. In addition, economic progress, together with the linking of production and consumption and the inevitable feedback between the two, the development of credit facilities and advertising have combined to raise both the standard of living and the individual's appetite for the amenities and benefits of the consumer society. However, it has become virtually impossible to satisfy this appetite without women participating directly in the economy. What is more, the uncertainty surrounding working careers as the result of the changes that are taking place in certain industries is encouraging families to safeguard their standard of living by means of two incomes. In order to satisfy needs that are now considered as normal, many families therefore require not only two incomes but also the provision of some form of care facilities for their children prior to their entry into the educational system. In many countries, the situation of the mother who does not go out to work is a vulnerable one, which no longer carries any particular social status and which places her in a position of material insecurity and dependence. This situation, which was considered normal a mere fifty years ago, has become the exception rather than the rule. In some countries, *e.g.* Denmark and Sweden, more than 80 per cent of women go out to work.

Thus, while the traditional tasks of the housewife have been simplified and automated to a considerable degree, her status has declined and lost much of its social prestige. Except in the case where it is a deliberate choice – generally where the husband's income is sufficient to support the family adequately – the women who do not go out to work are usually those who lack the requisite skills to qualify for a job or whose earnings would be too small to be of any real benefit. Sometimes women do not work through respect for traditional values whereby the mother has prime responsibility for bringing up the children, or because the number of children precludes the mother from working. It is a fact that labour force participation declines sharply in the case of women with three or more children.

A major feature of this trend leads to a somewhat paradoxical situation whereby the mothers who are available to look after their children are often those whose standard of education is the lowest and who, in addition, have to cope with difficult financial and material conditions due to the meagreness of the household's income. In many cases they suffer from social isolation and lack of self-esteem, sometimes resulting in social withdrawal and even physical debility which is detrimental to their relationship with their children. The children themselves may well be faced with a lack of stimulation, thus achieving less well educationally than those children in preschool. There may also be a depressing family atmosphere. They may also suffer from health problems, as evidenced by the increased use of medication, possibly as the result of a poor diet or a lack of immediate medical attention, or even be subjected to physical abuse – conditions which typify "at risk" status and can be precursors of school failure.

Child care facilities which could in principle help to compensate for these problems have not kept up with the obvious consequences of these trends, *i.e.* the need to devise alternative provision while mothers can supplement the family income via work. The establishment of *crèches,* kindergartens and nursery schools, which began in most countries during the latter part of the 19th century, has progressed very slowly. Although the pace may have quickened over the last twenty years in a few countries (*e.g.* Denmark, France, Sweden), in none are the facilities sufficient to meet the need.

Family structures

Family structures have changed considerably over the past few decades. Different generations no longer live under the same roof, which means that grandparents, for instance, are often no longer present to lend a hand or pass on knowledge and experience to younger generations.

The number of divorces has increased sharply, as has the number of lone parents. The emergence of "reconstructed" or "patchwork" families, with children from previous marriages, creates complex situations, the handling of which requires adequate financial resources and particular psychological and emotional skills. The children have to learn how to navigate between two households, to establish a relationship with their parents' new partners, their half-brothers or sisters and sometimes even with children who are not related to them in any way.

Although no research has been reliably able to demonstrate the potential harmfulness of such configurations, it is clear that, when parents do not have sufficient material and financial resources to allow the necessary adjustments (visits, suitable accommodation in each home), the children are affected by situations which are insecure and which are unable to provide them with the stability and regularity they require. Whenever the parents are unable to cope with the conflicts generated by separation, it is the children who suffer the emotional backlash. Here again, the adverse effects are accentuated by a low position on the socio-economic scale, particularly if the lone mother's socio-occupational level is not sufficient for her to take economic responsibility for her children. In the case of very young children, the problem of facilities for taking care of them while the mother is at work becomes crucial.

Socio-cultural

Life-styles, and particularly place of residence, have changed enormously. In many countries there has been a transition from an essentially rural existence to urban living, or rather suburban living, since it is the suburbs of major towns that have expanded so rapidly since the Second World War. The rural exodus, coupled with massive immigration from developing countries to richer countries where workers were in great demand, have created a shortage of housing in the major industrial centres.

During the three golden decades of post-war economic growth, the industrialised countries embarked upon wide-scale programmes for the building of low-cost housing. The aim in every case was to provide accommodation for the influx of people who were seeking a means of survival. Nowadays, they all present the same drawbacks: decay as a result of the poor quality of the materials, a lack of basic urban facilities (services, shops, meeting places), a ghetto atmosphere stigmatising their inhabitants who were the first to suffer the consequences of various economic crises that have followed one another since the 1970s. The children who grew up in these poverty-stricken environments now appear on the lists of the employment agencies. The cycle of poverty, instead of being broken, has become even more entrenched. The attempt to generalise access to education and training, which began with the raising of the school-leaving age, has failed, whereas progress in manufacturing industry in particular has led to the elimination of low-skilled workers and their replacement on a wide scale by robots to carry out simple, repetitive tasks. The persons hardest hit are obviously those who were unable to acquire specific occupational skills or whose qualifications have become outdated.

Although these neighbourhoods may have been inhabited by a fairly humble class of workers, they were able to survive and, more importantly, had established networks of mutual help and assistance with the added support of a common culture. They have subsequently become a mixture of different groups without the binding force and unity that time and a shared goal impart.

Governments have been slow in understanding the potential danger of these haphazard mixtures of population and the resentment and violence engendered by these inhuman living conditions. Countries are now giving much deeper thought to ways of improving conditions in their cities. Jobs, education and renovation have become key concerns as witnessed by the adoption of the poverty programme of the European social fund.

It is often in this sort of neighbourhood that children and youth "at risk" (CYAR) live. As far as very young children are concerned, it is frequently these neighbourhoods that are most lacking in *crèches* and childcare facilities. The nursery schools take in children from a very wide variety of social and cultural backgrounds, who are not used to the language of instruction, nor the cultural codes that prevail at school. The teachers are not properly trained to deal with the wide range of new situations with which they are confronted, particularly since schools generally operate on the principle of assimilation which may provoke opposition from parents on cultural grounds.

This resistance, sometimes conscious but more often unconscious, will not weaken unless the parents realise the advantages they could derive from active participation in guiding their child towards a destination, the characteristics of which they are in most cases unaware. The schools and *crèches* are not anxious to see their somewhat hermetic and well-regulated environment invaded by parents. And even when they are prepared to do so, the staff themselves are poorly paid and their schedule makes practically no provision for any such additional activity.

For various reasons many OECD Member countries are receiving increasing numbers of migrants who continue, quite naturally, bearing children. Within this general context, the status of the children is affected by issues surrounding the fact that they are members of the society of the host country. Recently in France, for example, the "droit du sol" (nationality conferred by birth within the country) has been challenged and there have been stormy debates about reintroducing the "droit du sang" (where the nationality conferred on the child is that of the father).

Furthermore, some immigrant women are not necessarily recognised by the social security system except through their children and it is through them that they acquire entitlement to certain welfare benefits. However, the rescinding of parental rights is one means of exercising control over family situations considered harmful to children. This potential sanction, which is seen as a threat (and occasionally used as one), has a considerable effect on the relationship between these families and social services. It can even deter them from seeking assistance in cases of genuine distress. It also exacerbates the atmosphere of mutual distrust, which often consequently vitiates the relationship between these families and workers from the socio-educational services.

Risks faced by young children exposed to such conditions

Risk factors likely to impact preschool children may derive from poverty, family instability (*e.g.* due to unemployment, substance abuse, lack of goal directness), isolation, child abuse and so on.

A number of health and psychological deficiencies are detectable right from the earliest checks. These fall into three broad categories and are outlined below.

A difference in functional capacity and standard of health

Many of the country reports include references to physiological handicaps, even though it may have been decided not to deal with this aspect as part of the detailed analysis. It is clear that, in addition to the numerous adverse effects of unfavourable living conditions, what also needs to be taken into account are the various functional handicaps that may afflict young children. Poor conditions of health and hygiene may be associated with problems ranging from auditory or visual impairments, mental dysfunctioning due to nutritional deficiencies, to alcohol or drug abuse during the mother's pregnancy, or even HIV infection which is currently one of the most common risks among children of mothers suffering from drug addiction.

Psycho-physiological disorders

- proneness to fatigue due to disturbed sleep patterns;
- gastric and intestinal disorders due to poor diet;
- psycho-motor retardation due to insufficient stimulation; and
- speech retardation due to the lack of interactions with others.

Syndromes resulting from disorganised mental processes

- systematically aggressive or lethargic behaviour;
- difficulties in communicating with other children or adults; and
- inability to concentrate or control motor functions.

Clearly, problems such as these can be detected only if the child is in contact with outside services during his early years (*i.e.* post-natal medical services) for example the health visitor in the United Kingdom, a *crèche* or similar establishment, a nursery school or some form of kindergarten. Unfortunately, it is the most vulnerable families that make least use of these services, unless they are free of charge, nearby and easily accessible, and providing there is no stigma attached to using these. In some cases, unless the problems are treated at a very early stage they can become irreversible, particularly those connected with the child's mental development.

Cultural handicaps

These psycho-physiological handicaps can be compounded by cultural handicaps:
- a mother tongue that is different from the language used outside the home;
- unfamiliarity with the basic instruments of early-learning processes (books, educational games and toys, the necessary means for getting physical exercise);
- play regarded as unnecessary and therefore not encouraged by the parents;
- the lack of supervision and rules preparing the child for life in a community (''children left to their own devices''); and
- a culturally structured family environment that is in contradiction or marked contrast with the education system's reference ''models''. This involves such aspects as the duration of the fusional relationship with the mother, the degree of freedom the children are allowed, their right of expression, the use of certain forms of punishment, the child's status and role in the sibling hierarchy (girl/boy, elder/younger) which are very closely interrelated in some cultures, etc.

These are all factors that condition children's ability to adjust to the universe they will encounter, including the age at which parents are willing to entrust their child to adults they do not know.

Aside from the fact that some children may not possess any of the cultural codes underlying the behaviour patterns of their peers, they may feel immersion in the school culture as a break, a rupture with the emotional content of the family environment. Depending on the nature of the family attitudes, children will either derive from school the resources that will stimulate their natural curiosity or feel left out or even rejected, since the school is not an environment where racism and segregation miraculously do not exist. If, to start with, the child has one or more of the above-mentioned handicaps, the risk of stigmatisation at an early age is very real and one that can only accentuate these handicaps.

Among factors that generate problems for a child, those all too often not mentioned are outside the family itself within the surrounding society. Different societies display different degrees of ostracism. Depending on the society's capacity to envisage and facilitate the integration of the more disadvantaged within the system, those children who have not had the advantage of being born in conditions conducive to their development will find themselves victims to a greater or lesser degree of misfortune in this respect. Democratic societies are based on the fundamental principle of equal rights. In practice, this principle is applied to a greater or lesser extent depending on the strategies adopted and with very different available means.

Prevention

Programmes that have been developed to ameliorate the circumstances of young children "at risk" have essentially a preventive intention. The importance of the first years of an individual's life to his later development has been sufficiently demonstrated by the research that has been carried out and so it is appropriate to use the term "prevention" in this context.

In order that programmes of prevention can be devised and put into operation, there are a number of necessary preconditions:

- the existence of infrastructures onto which they can be grafted;
- the requisite political will on the part of national and local authorities; and
- the allocation of financial resources that are both adequate and renewable on a long-term basis.

If these programmes are to be effective, there are a number of basic principles that need to be taken into account in the way they are planned:

- The child needs to be considered as a whole, which implies an interdisciplinary approach – the nutritional and health aspects, stimulation of the learning processes and the emotional aspects cannot be treated separately but only in a global way.

- The various risk factors mentioned above (unhealthy living conditions, uncertain economic survival, lack of outside social relationships, cultural differences, etc.) need to be addressed concurrently.
- Intervention must not relieve parents of their responsibility but rather reinforce it. Parents must therefore be closely associated with the educational processes and be given support in the form of information and the development of their skills.
- Children and their parents should, as far as possible, be assigned benefits that are ordinarily available rather than special measures which could have the negative effect of singling them out.

This implies that intervention programmes should be aligned as closely as possible on the local conditions in which they will be applied, rather than on imported models, and on the basis of detailed analyses of existing local resources and socio-economic and cultural contexts.

Infrastructures: an inventory

Given that most of OECD Member countries make little or no reference to the under-sixes in their reports, these do not provide all of the necessary elements for a comparison. It has fortunately been possible to supplement this information to some extent from the research literature as well as other sources such as the report "Who cares for Europe's children?" published by the Commission of the European Communities (Moss and Phillips, 1989), which of course covers only a limited number of OECD Member countries.

One of the first things that emerges is the fact that, for a very long time, strategies to remedy inequalities did not extend to under-school-age children. Whereas the education system in most industrialised countries was broadened to include all children towards the end of the nineteenth century, mother and child welfare provisions were not generalised (if at all) until after the Second World War.

Child care services were set up at the time when there was a substantial demand for women workers in major manufacturing complexes, with such facilities initially having strong connotations of being reserved for the less well-to-do classes. One of the main activities of these services was to provide basic health care in an attempt to reduce infant mortality. They developed very slowly and retained their down-market image throughout the 1960s and 1970s. Subsequently, a number of countries increased their efforts in this area substantially, investing in the construction of *crèches* and nursery schools. At the same time, these establishments benefited considerably from the discoveries regarding the development of the child and became very popular among the middle and upper classes. It was due to the pressure of the demand from these classes that the building programmes were stepped up. In those countries where this "move up-market" did not occur, there continues to be a lack of such services and those that exist are still, in theory, reserved for less well-to-do parents.

Whether or not a nation-wide programme exists, together with a system of regulations and supervision, depends on how centralised or decentralised the administration of a particular country is. Although free education has gradually become more widespread, albeit following widely different patterns (non-denominational schools funded by the State, subsidised denominational schools, non-fee paying systems for poorer students, etc.), *crèches* are still fee-paying. Income-related scales of charges go some way to establishing a balance but, in most cases, very poor parents are unable to find an affordable form of childcare.

The conditions applying in the case of working mothers differ widely from country to country in the following respects:

The length of pre-natal and post-natal maternity leave

The length of pre-natal and post-natal maternity leave that is allowed (from six weeks in the Netherlands to 14 weeks in Denmark) and the proportion of the cost borne by the State (from 70 per cent of earnings in Ireland to 100 per cent in Greece, the Netherlands and Portugal) vary substantially from country to country. The United States makes no provision in this area, for it is the responsibility of the woman herself to come to some arrangement with her employer regarding maternity leave. In some cases, she may have the right to reinstatement in her previous employment, but under certain conditions that are rarely fulfilled by those in low-skilled jobs.

The right to parental leave

The right to parental leave and some form of income during that period: only six EU countries have a provision regarding parental leave. In the case of four of these, financial support is also provided: 70 per cent of earnings in Denmark, 30 per cent in Italy, and fixed amounts in France and Germany. Sweden allows 12 months parental leave and a payment equivalent to 90 per cent of the earnings of either parent. This measure has had positive effects in terms of the birth rate and the involvement of fathers in the upbringing of their young children and has reduced substantially the demand for childcare services outside the home for children of this age.

Coverage of the demand for community facilities

Coverage of the demand for community facilities (*crèches,* childcare centres): in every country demand outstrips supply in the case of children under three, with coverage ranging from a figure of between 2 and 3 per cent in the Netherlands, the United Kingdom, Ireland and Luxembourg. It is closer to the average in Greece, the former Federal Republic of Germany and Spain. In France, Denmark and Italy this system is more extensive. In Sweden, under the terms of a decree adopted in 1985, the government undertook to provide total coverage for the demand. Even though this target has not yet been reached, the services currently cover about 80 per cent of the demand. In the United States, coverage has virtually doubled over the past ten years with some 40 000 centres serving 2.1 million children; 435 000 children are covered by a system of family day care but, as in most other countries, registered child minders represent only 10 per cent of the total number of women who look after children in their homes (Head Start Report).

Nursery schools and kindergartens

Nursery schools and kindergartens (for children from the ages of 2/3 up to 5/6 depending on the starting age for primary school) are more widespread, but their times of operation rarely correspond with normal working hours. Although in some countries the children attend full time with additional provision being made for the period both before and after normal hours, in others the children are allowed to attend only part-time for two to three hours a day.

The standards laid down

The standards laid down particularly regarding the qualifications of the staff, the adult/child ratio, space requirements, and medical and psychological monitoring vary from one country to another and from one system to another within the same country. The most common system is still that of family day care provided by a childminder, and it is also the one that is the least supervised, given that most child-minders are not registered. Professionals working in the preschool sector are generally very badly paid, even those who are required to have fairly high qualifications. These professions have a rapid turnover and tend to be chosen ''for want of anything better''.

A financial contribution from parents

All countries require a financial contribution from parents, during at least a part of the preschool period, although this is geared to parents' income. Some systems of childcare receive no government support whatsoever (non-registered childcare facilities), these being the most common and most widely available to disadvantaged families. Parents are usually little involved in the operation of these facilities and tend to be more in the position of consumers of a service, which can lead to a lessening of their commitment in terms of their responsibility for the child's upbringing.

The transition between the different settings in a child's life

The transition between the different settings in a child's life is not well or suffi-ciently organised. One reason why the transition from home to *crèche,* from *crèche* to nursery school and from nursery school to primary school is not well organised in some countries is that *crèches* and schools do not come under the same administrative authority (in particular, provision for the under-threes usually comes under the Ministry for Social Affairs or for Family Affairs, and that for 3 to 6 year olds under the Ministry of Education). What is more, in the case of families that are being monitored by social workers, the social workers may belong to yet another administrative department.

In short, most countries do not have sufficient broad provision to enable all parents, while they are at work, to place their children in a government-run establishment at a cost proportional to their means. This seriously jeopardises women's career prospects and may mean their having to give up work (which can undermine the household budget) and in some cases (for example, lone mothers) may even push them below the poverty line.

The non-availability or brevity of pre-natal and post-natal leave has repercussions on women's health and also on that of their children, as well as on the quality of the mother-child relationship (early abandonment of breast feeding and an undesirable and unduly early separation at a time of heightened psychological vulnerability). Conditions such as these are damaging to the whole of the infant population but are compounded, in the case of the more disadvantaged families, by the financial repercussions and those stemming from what are generally more tiring working conditions.

One of the first points that this report would emphasise, therefore, is the urgent need to review all of the provisions regarding childcare within our societies so that they reflect more closely present-day social realities. These provisions should be designed to provide the young children, irrespective of family background, with an environment suited to their needs, which can take over from the family whenever necessary and where the need for their parents to be present during a reasonable period following their birth is recognised.

Policy issues

What becomes apparent when one analyses the various policies to combat inequalities is that, for the most part, they are geared to strategies to counter their effects. Most welfare expenditure is devoted to programmes to combat delinquency, youth unemployment and educational underachievement. Preschool-age children are not, in most cases, among the concerns of policy-makers who consider investment in this area not only as very onerous but, where possible, to be avoided. This view is strongly conditioned by the dominant ideology in each country and in particular by what is considered to be women's role as opposed to the position they have been allowed to assume in the labour market (women's labour market participation rates are directly proportional to the quantity and quality of preschool provision). With the recession and rising unemployment in most industrialised countries, there is great temptation to brake women's entry into the labour market. This is given more or less clear expression depending on the political and economic approaches adopted at national and local levels.

From an ideological standpoint the debate is of little interest, since it would mean assuming that women still have a choice. However, the changes in habits regarding consumption and the lack of security in terms of stable employment and a stable marriage mean that women are virtually obliged to pursue a working career in order to ensure their continued economic survival. The idea that a women's place is in the home is changing, even though it is still widely accepted in countries like Germany, the Netherlands and the United Kingdom. In the United States it is forecast that the number of children under six with working mothers will rise from 49 per cent in 1985 to 65 per cent in 1995 (Department of Health and Human Services, 1990, p. 27).

Governments will henceforth need to consider very carefully the transfers of expenditure that will be necessary in order to cope with this irreversible trend, particularly since, with women increasingly gaining access to the same types of education and training as men, the younger generation will unquestionably be less willing to abandon their professional prerogatives. As for mothers who are finding entry into the labour market difficult, the consequences in terms of the financial costs of their social and economic problems in the long run are likely to place a far heavier burden on society than does the provision of childcare.

Financial resources

Depending on the type of welfare system in operation in each country, the family support services are to a greater or lesser degree financed out of public funds, with the result that their funding is subject to a greater or lesser degree of certainty. Various systems of public funding and private fund-raising exist alongside one another or may even be combined. In some countries public sector involvement is slight but an effective system of sponsoring by businesses has developed. In others, private sector funding is unusual and the services are publicly funded by central or local government out of what are fairly limited budgets.

In most cases the resources allocated are not sufficient, particularly for mounting large-scale projects with properly trained staff and providing a complete range of services. There are advantages and disadvantages with either system.

Private funding allows greater independence and more specifically targeted provision, but it means that those in charge of these services are constantly engaged in fund-raising activities which take up time and energy that could be better employed elsewhere.

Public funding means a regular income but less ability to adapt to particular situations which fall outside a predetermined framework. In Sweden, for example, when responsibility for *crèches* was transferred from central government to the municipal authorities, most of these complained that the standards laid down were too strict and often unsuited to the conditions in their area.

Without embarking on a systematic assessment of this aspect there are, nonetheless, a number of main points that can be made:

- A purely publicly funded system tends to shift the onus away from the rest of society and encourage a passive attitude on the part of parents and also of employers, thus lessening the pressure on policy-makers. It can also lead to a degree of inflexibility and uniformity in the solutions adopted, which may then prove to be ill-suited to local conditions.
- A purely privately funded system can result in considerable inequality in the resources allocated and in the quality of provision, make the services and the staff they employ very vulnerable, oblige their officers to engage in exhausting fund-raising activities and, lastly, shift the onus of responsibility away from the authorities.
- In every country we are beginning to see signs of a move towards a compromise solution and an attempt to strike a balance between the two systems, given the inherent drawbacks of each. This is certainly one of the more worthwhile avenues to explore.

Early intervention programmes for children "at risk": a brief description

The material that was collected from OECD Member countries did not yield a great deal of detailed information on practices with regard to preschool-age children. The description and commentary that follow will be confined primarily to the Report of the Head Start Evaluation Design Project (United States), the programme of Priority Education Zones (*Zones d'Education Prioritaire*) in France and the "Better Beginnings, Better Futures" project in Ontario (Canada) which are programmes intended for widescale implementation. In addition, we shall be looking at a number of smaller-scale experiments like those carried out in Winnipeg in the Province of Manitoba (Canada), Strathclyde (Scotland), Gelsenkirchen (Germany) and by the ACEPP (*Association des Collectifs Enfants-Parents-Professionnels*) in France – the last three of these projects were carried out by non-governmental agencies although they were partly government funded, with the government in each case taking a keen interest in the results.

Head Start (United States of America)

The main aim of the Head Start programme, launched in 1965, is to promote "the child's social competence" and at the same time to strengthen the family structure.

The programme is targeted primarily to "high risk" families of which two-thirds are ethnic minorities and 38 per cent black. Most of the children are between 4 and 5 years old. Some 1 900 centres managed by government agencies, community associations or schools cover a population of about 450 000 children throughout the country. Funding is allocated directly to local operators by the Federal government via the ACYF (Administration for Children, Youth and Family) on the basis of quality criteria. Considerable flexibility has been built into the programme so that individual projects can be adjusted to account for local conditions.

Each project can adopt one or more of the following methods of operation:

- five days a week full time or part time;
- only four days or less a week;
- on the basis of two groups of children, one in the morning and one in the afternoon;
- by arranging home visits combined with monthly sessions with small groups of children; and
- using methods designed locally for specific needs but subject to ACYF approval.

The Head Start programme has evolved as the result of periodic evaluations which are described in more detail later in this chapter. There have been four main stages in its development.

Stage 1 from 1965 to 1968: initially Head Start operated as a six- to eight-week summer programme covering 561 000 children in 2 400 different communities. The programme had difficulties in expanding its activities to cover a longer period because of the lack of available premises and staff, and financial problems.

Stage 2 from 1969 to 1972 is considered as having been a period of transition. The programmes became annual. Emphasis was placed on parent participation in the management of the centres, as paid or volunteer staff. ACYF's leadership set out to counter the threats to the programme's continued existence as the result of the findings of several evaluations. The so-called "Westinghouse Study", in particular, questioned the durability of the outcomes and the programme's cost-effectiveness.

Stage 3 from 1972 to 1977 was a period of improvement and innovation aimed at achieving the dual goals of child and family development. Vast efforts were put into planning and designing effective strategies. Guidance and monitoring techniques were devised, such as training programmes for the staff, a system of annual reports from field units, site visits and audits.

Stage 4 from 1978 to present has been a period of expansion on the basis of adjustments made during previous stages. Head Start covers one-fifth of the eligible population with a constantly increasing proportion of "high-risk families", partly as a result of the drive to recruit operators in disadvantaged neighbourhoods and partly as a result of the growing number of families affected by the economic crisis.

Head Start has served as a valuable source of inspiration for researchers and operators in the field of early intervention among young children. The discussions and judgements that it has given rise to have reached a wide audience as a result of the vast number of studies and analyses of the programme.

Zones of Educational Priority (ZEP) (France)

The ZEP programme, which was adopted by the French government in 1981 in an effort to reduce underachievement at school, was redefined in 1990. It is based on a socio-geographic approach which involves pin-pointing zones (with between 3 000 and 20 000 inhabitants) and formulating a policy of social intervention centred on the school but with the aim of bringing together various other services and agencies in a joint undertaking. The schools are allocated additional resources chiefly in the form of extra staff.

Most of these zones also receive assistance in the shape of operations for the "Social Development of Areas" (*Développement Social des Quartiers – DSQ*), which are a combination of structural renovation and socio-economic and cultural development projects. Within this framework, the programme as a whole is based on the concept of a partnership between the health, educational and cultural services, and between the decentralised services of central government and those of the local authorities. In principle, the inhabitants of the zone, through their associations, are involved in the planning and conduct of operations.

In ZEP the nursery schools, which generally take children from the age of three, have priority for the provision of care facilities for 2-year-olds if they belong to what is considered to be an "at risk" category. In the case of widespread intervention in a particular area, a number of firm recommendations have been drawn up regarding pre-school-age children, such as:

- "The cost of access to services and activities for the more disadvantaged sections of the community should be reduced or even eliminated entirely wherever possible."
- "Particular attention should be paid (...) to the provision made for young children."
- "These operations should focus on artistic and general cultural subjects, involving the parents and helping to raise the quality of the provision for the young child, its education, its socialisation and its ability to adjust to situations and life outside the family setting."
- "Co-operation between the staff of the schools and that of other agencies should be encouraged so that the children are not subjected to sudden or unduly sharp transitions."
- "Appropriate action should be taken with regard to parents and mothers in particular, especially where there is a need to provide instruction in the French language or literacy training."

[All quotes taken from the Ministerial document (February 1990) quoted in "The priority education area policy: a response to the children at risk problem".]

In order to qualify for the status – and the funding – of a ZEP, the schools are required to submit a project containing the original analysis of the situation, a plan of action (teaching strategies, methods of implementation, partners, resources available or required), methods of evaluation and a timetable covering three years.

A programme of evaluation is currently being carried out which was be completed in 1993. The case study submitted to CERI concerns the Alençon-Perseigne in the Orne department. This zone was chosen with a number of others as being typical of the type of action taken in a ZEP.

The number of ZEPs in operation during the academic year 1990-91 was 554, and this figure probably changed very little during the following year.

"Better Beginnings, Better Futures" project (Ontario, Canada)

This programme was launched on 13 November 1989 by the three ministries taking part in "Prevention Congress IV" (the Ministries for Community and Social Services, Education, and Health). It is planned that a longitudinal evaluation of the programme should be carried out over a period of 25 years and be based on two types of integrated services model:

i) prenatal/infant development programme integrated with a preschool; and
ii) integration of a preschool with a primary school.

The programme's goals are as follows:

- to prevent emotional, behavioural, social, physical and cognitive problems;
- to promote healthy child development; and

- to enhance communities (particularly by promoting initiatives for their economic and cultural development with a view to improving living conditions and restoring their self-esteem).

All of these strategies are based on the principle of integrating services so that they support one another, and on active participation by families and the community.

Depending on the particular situation in the community concerned, the task of coordinating the services has been assigned either to community agencies, community development groups, health units, or local schools and school boards.

The programme was launched in nine suburban communities in different cities and towns in Ontario; these communities are expected to develop their own models on the basis of the same set of predetermined goals and principles for the integration of services. By carrying out a comparative evaluation it should then be possible to identify appropriate strategies for attaining these goals.

"A School-Based Approach to Parent Involvement and Early Intervention" (Winnipeg, Manitoba Canada)

Victor Mager school is located in a suburb of Saint-Vital but has many of the characteristics of an inner-city school, being in an area where there is a high concentration of families facing economic difficulties and recent immigrants to the country, although 15 per cent of the school population are of aboriginal descent.

Its approach is based on a parent/school/community partnership. As part of its activities directed primarily to forging closer ties between the school and parents, it has launched a specific programme targeted to preschool children, "The Early Childhood Intervention Programme".

The aim of this programme, which is funded under the Manitoba Education and Training's Urban Compensatory Support Programme, is to enhance parents' education skills so that they can be of greater assistance to their children in the learning process. It provides learning opportunities for the children in which their parents take part. It has set up a resource centre where parents can familiarise themselves with the materials and games designed for the children. It provides sessions of training on early learning processes designed for both parents and staff working with young children.

The programme is intended to help parents to replicate at home the practices they see being used at the resource centre so as to prolong the beneficial effects of these on their children. The parent/school link is designed to:

- help parents to perform their educational role by providing them with the opportunity to learn about educational processes and by familiarising them with techniques they can use at home with their children;
- develop self-confidence among parents and children;
- encourage contact between parents and the staff looking after their children;
- develop a relationship of trust between parents and the school; and
- encourage the setting-up of a support network among parents so as to strengthen the cohesiveness of the community.

An interesting feature planned to be incorporated in the programme in the future is the involvement of high-school students as part of the practical experience required for their childcare courses.

This programme has been set up in three of the schools in Winnipeg attended by children who are considered to be "at risk".

"The Partnership in Education Project" (Strathclyde, Scotland)

Details of this project were submitted by the Bernard van Leer Foundation which is funding more than 100 early intervention projects in some 40 developed or developing countries throughout the world.

The project was launched in 1983 for a period of three years. It was subsequently extended for two further periods of three years in 1986 and 1989.

The initial objectives were as follows:

- create a supportive total environment to sustain the young child's growth and learning by activating local resources to achieve this;
- confirm the status of the parents as the child's prime educator, enhancing parents' understanding of their role in relation to the child's long-term development and affective stability;
- develop new working relationships between all statutory services and voluntary groups in an area, maintaining the child's effective learning through parent/child partnerships; and
- raise the educational levels of local children in an area.

The project's objectives during the subsequent two phases can be summarised as follows:

- the consolidation and handing on of the work carried out during the first phase;
- the replication of what was termed the "neighbourhood approach";
- the dissemination to other sites of the partnership approach both to working with parents and to interprofessional co-operation, using in-service training sessions with professionals as a mechanism;
- the clarification and documentation of the project's work and the expertise it had built up; and
- the development of relationships with other national and international networks in order to promote exchanges·and to ensure that the project's work be continued and sustained.

Once partnerships had been set up with parents and professionals, programmes of work were formulated making use of such facilities as preschool environments, primary schools, community buildings and local libraries. Activities included outings to places within the city or outside, and family activity holidays organised jointly by local professionals and parent groups.

The method of operation was based on constantly analysing and learning from experience – a "plan-act-reflect process". The principle was to develop parents' and children's abilities to solve a particular problem and plan the most suitable forms of organisation to promote the group's progress. This meant that these groups had to be small and function on a fairly regular basis.

According to the project's *rapporteur*, one of the reasons for the success of this mode of operation was the freedom and flexibility it allowed organisers to adapt their strategies in line with their observations of how these groups and local partnerships were developing.

Similar early intervention, based on the same principles, has been replicated in a number of other sites. The project has been contacted by other professionals who are anxious to be trained in the techniques of working in partnership with parents. The ''pilot'' sites continue to function but with only minimal supervision.

Türkische Kinder und Mütter (Gelsenkirchen, Germany)

The project, supported by the Freudenberg Foundation, and the van Leer Foundation, is located in a mining town in what was formerly West Germany, and one that has been hit by the recession affecting the industry as a whole. A large number of Turkish families and, more recently, Lebanese refugees live there alongside German families that are themselves facing socio-economic difficulties.

The project's basic purpose is to prepare Turkish children for school entry but, in addition, it includes activities aimed at mothers (literacy courses, German language courses, domestic science courses and leisure activities).

The children are given a year of pre-schooling in the primary school itself. Their monitor subsequently helps with their transition to first-year primary school by working together with the class teacher during the first few months. Mothers sit in on lessons so that they can more easily understand the learning processes. Sessions are also arranged for the purpose of encouraging parents to provide their children with educational support.

The emphasis is placed on the intercultural dimension of relationships both inside and outside the school, the idea being that, in the process of integrating immigrant families, the host society must also learn to be less categorical about cultural norms and assumptions.

The practice of questioning the validity of beliefs and prejudices about members of another culture is considered essential in order to arrive at a balanced view of the situation and avoid proposing ethnocentric and completely inappropriate intervention schemes.

The project attempts to put an end to the attitudes of resignation and apathy and restore to women both the desire and the power to take action with regard to their own lives. Another of its aims is to change the host society's views of specific cultural traits which frequently mask the similarities that exist between all human beings.

It also clearly sets out the limitations of intervention in general and of this type of intervention in particular: an attempt can be made to reduce the effects of risk factors, but if the situations in which the target groups for this intervention are ensnared do not change (and this is the crucial point as regards all of the problems mentioned above), the success of certain strategies over a longer period will very quickly be jeopardised.

Provision with parent participation for young children from culturally mixed and disadvantaged environments (France)

This project was launched in 1986. The ACEPP *(Association des Collectifs Enfants-Parents-Professionnels)* is an association which looks after and organises over 1 000 parent-run *crèches* in France. These crèches are managed and administered by parents who also take part in the day-to-day operation of these facilities in partnership with paid childcare professionals.

In 1986 a proposal for developing such facilities in disadvantaged areas received the approval and support of various ministries and the Bernard van Leer Foundation.

The philosophy underlying this project was that disadvantaged families should have the same possibilities as middle-class families of access to adequate childcare facilities for their children. Such facilities naturally provide a suitable environment for the pre-school training and socialisation of children, virtually all of whom – in France – enter nursery school at age 3 or even 2 in some cases (see the section above on ZEPs).

Parents' participation in the educational process at these *crèches* provides a means of easing the cultural transition between the home and life at school, and also helps to teach parents about assuming their responsibilities vis-à-vis their children. The parent group becomes a mutual support unit. It also means that mothers can either go to work or take a training course so as to increase the family income. Participation in the running of these *crèches* is an exercise in civic responsibility and one which enables them either to acquire or further reinforce their personal autonomy.

The aim of combating underachievement is obviously linked to the process of familiarising the children with the language and the cultural codes of behaviour in relation to their own parental culture. The entire approach is based on the quality of the partnership between parents and the professionals, who receive regular in-service training in this connection. All of this takes place either in premises that have been set up for this purpose (under the legal and financial conditions governing parent-run *crèches*) or within existing *crèches* where this participatory approach has been adopted.

Following a three-year pilot phase, the scheme is now being extended more widely. More than 25 centres have been set up, most of them in areas designated for a DSQ or "neighbourhood social development" scheme (see the section above on ZEPs). They form part of a campaign to combat the various risk factors and are one of the many forms of partnership in which the agencies of both central and local government work together. The link between *crèche* and nursery school is established through co-operative undertakings mainly involving general cultural subjects.

Summary of the essential features of these programmes

From an analysis of these programmes it is clear that they have a number of common features, namely:

    i) The importance placed on the early learning processes and the socialisation of the child in order to provide the proper basis for its subsequent development. The aim is to prepare the child for school life but other factors are taken into account, in particular the child's emotional balance and physical health which, while they may affect academic performance, are not causally related to cognitive skills (many highly strung children perform perfectly well at school and dental decay has no direct effect on the brain). There is frequent reference to "global development" as the means of preserving the natural assets inherited at birth.

ii) The vital role of parents in the educational process. A child's emotional balance is closely governed by its relationship and its identity vis-à-vis its parents. Most of the programmes therefore provide for parent participation in the activities arranged for the child in order that they should realise what is at stake, to help them use similar educational methods and approaches at home, and to rebuild or reinforce their feeling of competence and their sense of responsibility.

iii) The move away from preconceived models and towards more individualised approaches in the formulation of which the parents are involved and which are based on a realistic assessment of the situation and the potentialities of the environment. It was recognised that the "passivity" of the "clienteles" for social intervention is often a reaction to the lack of consultation when programmes are being planned and of involvement when they are being set up.

iv) The attention devoted to transitional stages (between the home, preschool facilities and the primary school), so as to prevent the cultural shocks that can occur particularly in the case of children belonging to a very different cultural environment from the surrounding one. Most of the programmes operate in conjunction with or even within schools – the most difficult task frequently being that of changing the habits and attitudes of teachers.

v) The more global approach to situations and contexts with the aim of improving the child's and the family's living conditions, particularly by means of individual development strategies to provide the parents with opportunities for education and training, access to the labour market, better housing, regular health checks, etc., and community development strategies to promote mutual help and support and build up a social and relational network. All of the programmes include provision for social "get-togethers".

vi) Awareness of the training needs of the staff working with children and parents, many of whose initial training did not cover all of the aspects and problems encountered in practice.

vii) The partnership approach and the integration of services: those involved often have specialist rather than all-round skills. In addition, they belong to different services which come under different government departments and budgets (i.e. health, labour, education, housing, immigration in some cases, the various local authorities, etc.), all operating at different levels in a manner which may vary in its form from country to country but not in its complexity. In order to avoid a dispersal of effort and ensure that all of the needs can be addressed, programmes should therefore be planned within a framework which ensures that the services provided are complementary to one another. This ideal arrangement is, of course, greatly hampered by bureaucratic habits and the political and institutional rivalries that "enliven" the routine of daily life.

The issues discussed above reflect features that are common to all of the projects analysed. One of the points on which they differ is the question of integration which, in fact, is central to the strategies employed to prevent children from becoming marginalised. This raises problems of approach and consequently calls into question systems that have been designed for this purpose. This may be readily illustrated by contrasting the approaches of English and French speaking countries.

The traditional approach in English-speaking countries recognises cultural differences and the communities that emerge as a result. The traditional approach in French-speaking countries, which is more assimilative in character, regards membership of a country as taking precedence over membership of an ethnic group. This gives rise to fairly different models in terms of integration strategies. In the first case, intervention schemes among ethnic minorities will be firmly based on the communities that have been formed whereas, in the second case, such schemes will have to conform to a principle of non-segregation and be set in the context of a cultural mix, otherwise they will be considered stigmatising in their effects. In France, it was not until 1983 that the right of association was extended to foreigners. Government funds are rarely allocated to projects whose sole outcome would be to promote the cultural self-sufficiency of their members.

This difference in the cultural background helps to explain why projects in English-speaking countries tend to take these communities as their starting point and attempt to encourage them to increase their openness and representation in the outside world, whereas projects in French-speaking countries tend to start from a common core and create openings and allow access to individuals from cultural minorities.

Lastly, one important aspect is the size of these programmes. In the examples available, the schemes have been carried out within the context of an entire country (Head Start in the United States, the ZEPs and parent-run *crèches* in France), a province (Ontario, Manitoba), a region (Strathclyde) or a town (Gelsenkirchen). One thing they all have in common, however, is that they demonstrate the methods that are used and how these are evaluated from the standpoint of their application on a wider scale.

The differences between them are due essentially to two key elements.

Who initiated the programme?

In the case of the United States and France, the decision to launch the programmes was taken at the central government level. In the case of Ontario and Manitoba, it was taken by the provincial government. In other cases, they are local initiatives run by private bodies which nevertheless rely on public funds to support such schemes although they have not been directly initiated by government services. The procedures are therefore designed on a smaller scale.

Whereas central government is able to mount large-scale schemes (2 400 sites for the launch of Head Start and 544 ZEPs), the scope of local programmes is obviously more limited, while those run by private bodies usually start off with just a few or even only one pilot operation. The aim is still replication on a wider scale but, in this case, the strategies are not the same.

In the case of nation-wide schemes, the evaluations that are carried out are intended not only to assess cost-effectiveness but, more importantly, to refine the methods currently in use, notwithstanding the fact that the underlying aim may be to extend the scheme, particularly by means of statutory provisions (making it compulsory for all childcare and preschool facilities to apply the methods in question).

Local programmes are evaluated with the same aim of application on a wider scale, the only difference being that the number of experiments available for analysis is naturally smaller. In this case, therefore, one of the main aims is to assess the effectiveness of the methods used on a small scale, how they have worked in different contexts and how applicable they would be on a broader scale. The process of evaluation is directly connected with the need to ensure continued financial support for the project and serves as a means for defending the interests of the programme itself.

One of the major differences is the amount of money that can be spent on evaluation. This can have an effect in terms of the type of evaluation procedures used, with the usual opposition between internal and external evaluation, the latter rarely being affordable in the case of smaller-scale projects.

The time factor

The type of evaluation carried out is dictated to a large extent by the age of the project, with longitudinal studies being appropriate only in the case of programmes that have been in operation for some time. This is clearly indicated by the fact that, in the case of the documents that were submitted in this connection, only those concerning the Head Start programme included a wide range of research reports. The ZEPs have undertaken a quantitative evaluation, the results of which were not available when this report was written. The corresponding qualitative evaluation covers only 12 zones and the French report mentions only one of these. In contrast, the other case studies provide a far more detailed description of aims and methods than of evaluation.

Some general observations based on the evaluations

From the outset, the Head Start operation made research and evaluation a key element in the process of developing and improving its programmes. More than 1 600 research reports have been compiled, although their potential has so far been under-utilised. A network of 14 university-based research centres collected information over the period 1966-69 and compared this with other types of intervention which had had fairly positive outcomes.

The Westinghouse Study, the main aim of which was to determine to what extent the progress achieved by the children was maintained after the first and second years in primary school, was for a long time considered the classic study on Head Start. Its findings seemed to indicate that the effect of Head Start was not very significant and that it faded after the second year in primary school. This study, whose methods subsequently received some very severe criticism by the consortium which rejected their arguments, nevertheless had a very serious impact on the further development of the programme in the short term. The value of Headstart is now widely recognised and much additional funding has been made available.

It would be impossible here to quote all of the studies that have been carried out on Head Start or including Head Start as one of several preschool projects analysed. Both the aim and emphasis of these studies differ widely. A few examples will illustrate the complexity of the data and types of research:

- primarily, of course, what children gained from the programme, but also;
- the external, contextual factors that influence a child's development and the early learning processes;
- factors in the child's family background that affect these processes;
- a comparison between centre-based (Head Start) programmes and home visit programmes (Home Start);
- comparison of curricular models; and
- analysis and synthesis of different research reports using the techniques of meta-analysis.

Lastly, the results that different reports have provided have not necessarily been based on an analysis of the same elements.

However, from all of these studies and evaluations a number of broad conclusions can be drawn which are common to them all, notwithstanding the specificity of the programmes and the methods of analysis used.

The children

The children who attended early intervention programmes benefited from them, as is demonstrated by the assessments made both during and after these programmes. The findings show an improvement in their linguistic, cognitive and physical skills; in their sociability, and particularly their ability to communicate with their peers or with adults; in their readiness for school; in their heightened self-confidence and greater maturity; and in their generally better health as a result of the medical and nutritional supervision they received during the course of the programme. It is difficult to say whether these effects are long-lasting, given the fact that, in most cases, virtually no longitudinal studies have been carried out (apart from a few that have only recently been launched) and given that their methods are still somewhat tentative. The degree and nature of parents' involvement has a profound impact on a child's progress.

Organisational models

As far as the professionals' training is concerned, this is a question not so much of its level and duration but its content. An overly formal or overly general pre-service training may be less useful than forms of in-service training based on everyday experience. The amount of work experience within a programme or a similar setting is a very important factor.

The approaches compared have all been identified as examples of "good practice". It is therefore perhaps not surprising that, providing parents and professionals work together in harmony, there is little to choose between the programmes selected.

The child/adult ratio is a key factor: the lower it is (four or five children per adult) the better the results.

Flexibility in meeting child and family needs is essential to the effectiveness of programmes.

The families

Programmes that include providing support for parents (home visits, family evenings, training for parents, workshops, language or literacy courses, skills training) are more successful in persuading parents to participate in the activities arranged for their children. Parent participation cannot be made mandatory, it requires the right kind of approach that takes into account the degree and nature of parental involvement while at the same time encouraging and supporting their efforts. Parents' fears and misgivings have to be taken into consideration. And what professionals need, in addition to organisational skills with regard to a group of children, are relational skills with regard to their parents.

The communities

Professionals working with "at risk" groups need to have the ability to question the doctrines and assumptions that, consciously or unconsciously, govern their actions. To quote the words of Carmen Treppte (*Türkische Kinder und Mütter*, Gelsenkirchen): "Irritatingly enough, we found ourselves in the role of those who learn by seeing our own values and concern reflected in the mirror of a different culture (which made them rather ridiculous at times)".

"At risk" groups cannot be characterised solely in terms of their belonging to a cultural minority. Their economic status is a far more significant factor and one that marginalises them more surely than membership of an ethnic minority. However, those projects that are designed to encourage the preservation of the symbols of cultural identity are more likely to be successful. Preserving the individual's mother tongue and encouraging parents to use it with their children facilitates acquisition of the majority language (ACEPP).

Encouraging community participation in preschool programmes is a good way of encouraging strategies of self-reliance and local development and the positive effects that these have in improving the child's environment.

At one of the sites for the project "Provision for Young Children from Culturally Mixed Environments" in France, playground equipment was built for children from *crèche* age upwards with the help of the local townspeople, and this is used by all of the children from the youngest to the oldest. In Strathclyde, the programme arranged group holidays at the seaside and in the country.

The partnership principle

All of the programmes considered have been designed from the outset with the idea of a partnership between the various local services or associations. Either the programme's legal and financial structure is itself based on a partnership, *i.e.* several ministries and/or local government departments will share the costs and make available resources in terms of services and staff, or a separate operation within a programme will set up a partnership as the best means of achieving its objectives. In either case, the pooling of skills and resources is the most effective way of achieving the programme's aims and particularly for embarking on a process that encourages the widespread implementation of its programme.

The techniques of communication and gaining media attention are aspects which need to be incorporated in the planning:

- communication within the projects so as to get the participants thinking, and communication directed to parents to encourage them to participate and become involved in the educational activities;
- external communication directed to policy-makers, researchers and practitioners concerned by the type of experiment being carried out; and
- gaining media attention with the object of making a wider public more aware of the whole question of preschool education.

These techniques are obviously an excellent way of building up a meaningful and dynamic partnership as the strongest form of support for the project as a whole.

Cost effectiveness

Not enough studies have been done that would enable a comparison between expenditure on early intervention and the long-term savings this may have yielded in terms of expenditure on welfare, combating underachievement at school, preventing juvenile delinquency, unemployment benefits and so on; although the well known evaluations of the Perry preschool programme do demonstrate the cost benefits of compensatory preschool education on exactly these variables (Barnett, 1992).

However, economies of scale are possible provided that a few basic principles are adopted:

- making use of existing facilities by arranging preschool provision on their premises (*e.g. crèches* operating on school premises, using community facilities, libraries, health centres, home visiting, etc.); and
- involving parents in activities on a voluntary basis so as to have a satisfactory child/adult ratio and reduce staffing costs at the same time. However, this reason on its own would be unacceptable were it not for the fact that parents' involvement is of educational benefit to both the child and parent. Nonetheless, the professionals should be paid an adequate salary in line with the high level of skills required.

Conclusions

Early intervention is the corner-stone of any social system that seeks to guarantee its members maximum opportunities for individual and collective fulfilment. The complete elimination of differences and inequalities is no doubt an unrealistic, not to say unattainable, aim. Nonetheless, it is clear that a society that does not take pains to offset and level the effects of the social and economic inequalities within it runs the risk of splitting asunder.

Children represent the human potential that will ensure the country's future. The expenditure allocated for preserving and developing this potential must therefore be considered as a priority within the country's budget. At a time when the management of resources has to take into consideration the interdependence of economics and ecology, investment in education takes on all of its significance as a basic prerequisite for the progress that humanity can still hope to accomplish for itself.

Keypoints

The first few years are paramount

It is now widely recognised that the first few years of life can be a critical part of successful future development both in school and in societal integration.

Review of provisions regarding child care

Child care provision is in urgent need of review in order to reflect more closely present day social realities. Provision should be designed to provide young children, irrespective of background, with an environment suited to their needs.

The new expectations of women

Careful consideration will need to be given to the transfer of expenditures necessary to cope with women's new and irreversible aspirations to continue to develop their professional careers.

A balance needs to be struck between public and private funding for child care

Both purely public and purely private funding of child care has its disadvantages. In many countries there are moves to find a compromise and further exploration is urgently needed.

Emotional, physical and cognitive factors must be taken into account in early childhood programmes

In order to establish a proper basis for later learning and development it is essential to emphasise the place of early learning and socialisation and to take special account of emotional and health as well as educational factors.

Parents play a vital role in the educational process

Parent participation is essential in effective early education programmes.

Programmes should be individualised and consultative

In order to avoid passive acceptance or rejection, programmes should not be preconceived but individualised to meet the child's needs in consultation with parents.

Attention needs to be given to transitional periods

To avoid the cultural shocks that occur when moving from home to school, close attention needs to be given to the transition phase. Teachers in particular need to be especially sensitive.

The family needs support too

To improve the conditions for the child, the family also needs to have improved access to education and the labour market.

Staff need training

The importance of appropriate staff training cannot be over-emphasised. There is a need to emphasise practical experience.

Partnership and the integration of services

Services should be co-ordinated and complementary and should see each other as partners and not as rivals.

Teacher/adult-pupil ratio is crucial

Four to five preschool children to each adult represents a goal to be aimed for which may be achieved by utilising parents constructively.

Being sensitive and responsive to cultural identity is crucial

Programmes that work pay attention to the symbols of cultural identity and professionals must be prepared to challenge and reinterpret their own assumptions and actions in the light of different cultural values.

Economies of scale

Cost-effectiveness can be achieved through economies of scale such as the creative use of already existing provision and by involving parents to improve adult-child ratios. Cost-benefit analyses reveal long-term gains following certain preschool programmes.

References

BARNETT, S.W. (1992), "Benefits of compensatory preschool education", *The Journal of Human Resources*, Vol. XXVII, pp. 279-312.
Department of Health and Human Services (1990), "Final report of the Headstart Evaluation Design Project", mimeo, Office of Human Development Services, Contract No. 105-89-1610.
MOSS, P., and PHILLIPS, A. (1989), *Who Cares for Europe's Children*, EC, Brussels.

Country Case studies
Australia: Interagency referral process: a mechanism for integrating health, education and welfare services for school-aged children and adolescents with social and behavioural difficulties.
Canada (Ontario): Better Beginnings, Better Futures.
Canada (Winnipeg): A school-based approach to parent involvement and early intervention.
France: *Zones d'Education Prioritaire*.

Foundation case studies
ACEPP and van Leer (France): Provision with parent participation for young children from culturally mixed and disadvantaged environments.
Freudenberg (Germany): *Türkische Kinder und Mütter*.
Van Leer (United Kingdom): The partnership in education project.

Chapter III

Changing Schools

by

Philip Williams
University of Wales

Background

The case studies reviewed in this chapter deal with the ways in which schools in OECD Member countries are developing approaches to educating children and youth "at risk" (CYAR). These studies are listed at the end of the chapter.

The reports describe a rich variety of educational explorations. Few reports are complete, for most are studies of innovatory developments which were current at the time the reports were written. Most are not controlled experiments, but evolutionary activities, often with their own momentum and with unforeseen consequences. For these reasons, few of the evaluations are cast in the traditional mould, exemplified by control-group, experimental-group comparisons. Most appraisals are on-going, formative evaluations describing findings and offering comments at different stages of a programme's development.

The reader of these case studies cannot fail to be struck by their honesty. Reports have not shirked from pointing out weaknesses as well as successes. Not all innovations have succeeded and even where there is general and considerable satisfaction with a programme the reports often make the point that overall success does not imply success over all.

In this chapter the scene is set with a short section on "The school: success or failure?". Three sections then deal with reforms covering the curriculum, new educators and reorganisation, respectively. This is followed with a section titled "Signals from the case studies", commenting on the salient points which have emerged. A concluding section summarises the findings in a short series of simple recommendations.

The school: success or failure?

It is now well over a hundred years since compulsory education for all children – elementary at first – became a characteristic of developed societies. With few exceptions, children were brought together and taught together in large groups or classes, usually of similar ages. Several classes formed an institution which was to appear in every village, town and city: the school. The idea of a school was not new, for schools of a kind had existed from early history. But what was new, for most OECD countries, in the later decades of the nineteenth century was the idea that childhood education should be provided for all. The school, with its high pupil-teacher ratio and the economic advantages deriving from size was then the most efficient – if not the only – way of ensuring that all were educated. The existence of a system of schools in every centre of population, large or small was a mark of an advanced society.

As the twentieth century progressed, so the pressures for more education swelled, fuelled on the one hand by the belief that education was an essential tool for providing a more highly-skilled population, and on the other by the belief that education was an intrinsic good to which everyone had a right. The proponents of these alternative arguments debated what should be taught: but they also formed an uneasy alliance which for different reasons called for the age limit of school attendance to be extended. At suitable moments that call was heeded, so that today many developed countries expect all their children and young people to attend school or college until their late teens. It can be argued that the educational policies of the first half of this century have rested on the belief that "more means better" and have been devoted more to changing the length of school experience and less to changing the nature of that experience.

Recently, this earlier belief in the value of education provided in and through school has been more carefully examined. Helvetius's view that "*l'éducation peut tout*" has been regarded as an idealistic over-simplification. Disenchantment has led to more open criticism of the steady growth in the time children spend at school and to the increasing cost of this expansion. The arguments raised against education in school are in fact not new: they echo those that were heard over a century ago when countries were debating the introduction of compulsory education.

What are these criticisms? They are criticisms based on disappointment – disappointment that the education process, notwithstanding the resources provided, seems unable to prevent some school-leavers entering society with poor attainments, antisocial behaviour, unreasonable expectations and a general reluctance to participate in constructive activity: in short the many issues mentioned in the introduction. The uneasy alliance that advocated, for different reasons, the growth of schooling, now divides to criticise it from different standpoints.

One group of voices deplores the drop in standards, both of attainment and of behaviour. In particular, these voices argue that current attempts to offer a long, common educational experience to all children has led to a dilution of that "thin clear stream of excellence" without which society will not progress. Extended education should be restricted to the minority who can benefit.

Another group disagrees. Its members argue that the educational experience usually on offer is inappropriate for a different reason. They argue that it is not length and availability, but content that is at fault. For many pupils, the school curriculum is too heavily academically weighted, and has thus contributed to the alienation that young people with poor attainments and antisocial behaviour show.

These are complex matters which it is easy to over-simplify. It is easy to over-emphasise the role of school in an intricate learning process which heavily involves the family in particular, and other influences too. The media explosion in general and television in particular, affect children's learning – including behaviour patterns. Some of the criticisms, *e.g.* those of poor standards, may be based on selective measurements.

But whatever the cause, most politicians in most governments recognise the existence of the problems identified in the Introduction – the existence of ''at risk'' children and young people. Country reports demonstrate that these concerns are common across the OECD Member countries irrespective of variations in educational policies. There is a call for change in the educational experiences we offer. So the question to be addressed in the rest of this chapter is: what changes help schools to deal with their ''at risk'' pupils?

Curriculum reform

If by some supernatural process, one of the great 19th century educators were to visit a fairly typical modern school, he or she would find many differences. The dramatic drop in class size would immediately strike the educator. The replacement of slate and pencil by the generous diversity of modern teaching equipment would be a source of wonder. The change in role of the head teacher, no longer a teacher but a manager of an enterprise, would be a surprise. But the routine of lessons, the engine of education, would occasion little surprise. Much of the content of the lesson material itself would also be clearly and immediately recognisable. True, the classics would probably be absent, replaced by either another foreign and/or computer language. Technology lessons would be identified as the old woodwork and metalwork, metamorphosed. But from the early emphasis on the basic skills of reading and number to the later introduction of the subjects of history, geography, languages and science, much would be familiar.

Curricular change is slow. It is affected by the very human reluctance of some educators to throw away the smooth sequences of their old established lessons and to take on the chore of learning different practices, aiming at different targets. It is also governed by an unspoken fear of redundancy in teachers whose specialism may be threatened. But change does take place. Take one vivid example. In the 15th century, a student wishing to learn how to add and subtract was advised to attend an Italian university, whereas for multiplication and division, the German universities were better. By the end of the 19th century, with the demand for a numerate population, the conceptual difficulty of these symbolic operations was ignored and they were and are regularly taught to all in the early years of the primary school. Computer programming, which has undergone a similar (and much faster) introduction into schools, is another, contemporary example of curricular change. In other words, resistance to curricular change can be overcome, given the will. One approach is through setting national targets.

Comprehensive national change

If the school is the convoy which children join in order to develop into adults, then the curriculum is the road along which they journey, traversing various landscapes on the way. It is by changing the route and insisting on a specific destination that their experiences can be altered and their preparation improved. Some of the countries in this project have aimed to improve the educational standards of all children by setting specific destinations, or targets for everyone. Thus the United States reported a set of national educational goals expressed as voluntary examinations in five core subjects for children aged ten, fourteen and eighteen. The programme is incentive-led with rewards to individuals and schools who excel in progress towards the programme's targets (ref. 1*).

In the United Kingdom, a National Curriculum has been introduced with similar intentions (ref. 2). It differs from the American model in that national tests are set at different ages, starting as early as seven. They cover a wider range of subjects and are compulsory. Rewards are less obvious but are undoubtedly present for test results are published by school, parents can choose to send their children to more effective schools and school funding is largely driven by pupil numbers.

These are examples of significant national efforts to raise educational standards for all. Although these major reforms are not directed specifically towards "at risk" children it is intended that these children too will have their standards of achievement lifted alongside those of their fellow pupils.

When national curricula are prescribed, there is a danger that they will emphasise academic subjects: indeed the main aim of such exercises is usually to raise the academic standards of the school population. Moreover, it is relatively easy to set achievement targets by subject. Many argue that this is a very narrow view of the purpose of education. Children learn – or should learn – much more at school than skills with mathematical symbols, historical knowledge, or foreign languages, for example.

This is not to deny the importance of such subjects. But there are so many other ways in which schools help their pupils. The development of social and moral values, such as awareness of others' rights, tolerance, respect for the law – qualities such as these are essential for citizenship; they are encouraged in a successful school community.

It is often argued that these are qualities which should be fostered by the family. This is indeed so. But when families are feckless, irresponsible, and stressed, children are unlikely to learn properly these social and moral values at home. The school then becomes ever more important. Academic standards should not be sought at the expense of other, less easily quantifiable standards. To put it another way, attitudes are as important to society as attainments.

---

* The numbers in brackets refer to documents mentioned in the references at the end of the chapter.

The reading and language curriculum

Some countries describe curricular reforms pointed directly towards the "at risk" population. In several cases, early competence in reading, the key to curricula which are everywhere still heavily dominated by the printed word, has been recognised as of over-arching importance. Thus Marie Clay's Reading Recovery programme, which originated in New Zealand, has been introduced into a number of US schools, with positive results (ref. 3a). This programme aims to catch children "at risk" of reading failure as young as six years. The case study reports positively on the progress of pupils and the enthusiasm shown by the teachers and schools involved. The programme, which differs from most previously introduced remedial reading programmes through its emphasis on starting help early, before bad reading habits develop, has since been introduced into the United Kingdom, with government support.

The Canadian material describes a modification of the Reading Recovery programme, a reading/writing immersion project, used in the first grade of three high-need elementary schools in Winnipeg (ref. 4b). Evidence from the teachers involved also stresses the positive outcomes.

A Portuguese project is based on primary schools in run-down areas of Lisbon (ref. 5a). It has several different objectives, one of which is to develop pupils' oral and written communication skills. This is based on the view that "children from cultures habitually held in low regard (i.e. ethnic minorities and the disadvantaged) can be taught reading and writing skills in the same period of time as other children, provided new practices and pedagogical attitudes are adopted".

This project has several interesting features. It proceeds through four preliminary stages, designed to tap the knowledge and secure the interest and commitment of those teachers who intend to participate in the project. The programme does not rely on modifications or adaptations of existing materials, but uses the child's own experience as the basis for developing individualised teaching materials, aimed at enhancing language and reading. As in other programmes, regular teacher meetings, in this case led by teacher-counsellors, provide the stimulus for programme development, which is thus teacher-led, with support from central government.

A French case study, though it is concerned with preschool children, should be mentioned, for unlike other projects, this focuses on improving one specific language area, of particular relevance to children "at risk", i.e. the language of the school (ref. 6a). The importance of competence in and familiarity with the communication medium of education could make a significant difference to the critical first experience of school.

A report from the Netherlands describes a reading programme with a different theme (ref. 7). The reading promotion programme introduced in Utrecht aims at enhancing children's motivation to read, rather than boosting their reading attainment as such. The reading promotion activities involve not only the school, but also the local library and the community centre. The programme emphasises the importance of the correct selection of books, of their presentation to children so as to arouse interest, and of increasing a child's familiarity with class, school and local library. The case study reports the successful results achieved with the nine to twelve year olds attending schools in an educational priority area. Pupils in the reading promotion programme are better motivated to read, particularly to read for its own sake. There is also evidence that they read more often. This report triggered a broad reading motivation programme in the Netherlands for its whole school age range financed by the Ministry of Welfare, Health and Culture.

These case studies illustrate the various ways in which countries are experimenting successfully with improving reading and language skills of "at-risk" children, mainly in the early years of schooling. Other case studies illustrate projects which also concentrate on this phase, but with a broader curricular focus.

The basic subjects

In case studies of projects concentrating on improving attainments in the basic subjects, reading success is again an important target, though not the sole one. The United States contribution includes a report on the "Success for All" (SFA) project, initially in operation in disadvantaged schools in Baltimore (ref. 3b). This project aims to ensure that all children are given the necessary teaching to enable them to achieve the norms in basic skills set for grade three level by the time they are in grade three, arguing that children who fail in these early years are those who later drop out and show the characteristic problems of the "at risk" groups described in the introduction.

It is an eclectic project, utilising any research that has demonstrated an effective contribution to educational achievement. Broadly, the programme exploits well-tried language development techniques such as the Peabody programme, followed by an intensive beginning reading programme with a phonic emphasis, reflecting current views on the value of such techniques for children with reading difficulties. The reading programme itself involves co-operative reading activities, the students working in pairs and teams on activities directed towards vocabulary building and comprehension, presumably grounded on the reported effects of peer tutoring. Students receive an hour and a half of reading tuition each day, in groups of fifteen to seventeen, arranged by performance level, not age.

The maths component is taught through a similar mixture of co-operative learning experiences and group instruction. Like the reading programmes, maths is followed up by the individual tutoring that the remedial programme of earlier decades utilised. Pupils who need extra instruction receive twenty minutes of individual tutoring each day. In addition, reading progress is assessed every eight weeks, a less frequent assessment than some programmes would advocate, but nevertheless reflecting the value attached to regular measurement of progress.

These extensive modifications to the basic curriculum are accompanied by a teacher-training component and by teams of family support workers, issues to which we return later in the chapter.

Not all programmes aiming at the basic subjects are introduced in the early school years. The Comprehensive Competency Programme (CCP) is a United States-wide scheme, providing learning centres for disadvantaged youth (ref. 8). In these centres the emphasis is on language and maths skills, and on functional competencies. They are based in community facilities such as job centres, and in secondary schools. More recently, some have been located in junior high schools. In early 1991, 15 per cent of students attending CCP centres were under the age of fifteen.

An example of a setting where this programme is in operation is provided by the Hoover School in San Diego. Here, there are some two thousand students on roll, of whom nearly a half leave each year, to be replaced by more immigrants. Twenty-seven different languages are spoken in the school, and English is a second language in 60 per cent of the homes.

The CCP provides courses which include a strong computer-based element, leading to individualised instruction; they use the principles of assessment and feedback that are characteristic of mastery learning. The evaluation of the programme mentions average gains of well over a year's progress for thirty-plus hours of tuition in both reading and maths. In one location, referral to the CCP is used as one treatment for truancy.

The CCP offers in all over twenty different courses. As well as those covering reading, language and mathematics, others cover a variety of social and pre-employment skills. This element in the programme leads us to examine innovations which aim to alter the traditional curriculum, rather than emphasise improving the level of attainment in the basic subjects.

A more relevant curriculum

Other case studies are specifically aimed at curricular changes in later school years. There the target is to provide a more relevant curriculum. The word "relevant" in relation to the curriculum has led to considerable debate, the argument largely revolving around the view that there is a sense in which any educational activity can be regarded as relevant to something! In answer to the question "relevant to what?" the response of these "at risk" programmes is usually "relevant to later careers". One Portuguese case study, the Inter-ministerial Programme for Promoting Success in Education (PIPSE), aimed for a drastic re-education in educational failure through introducing, among other measures, major structural reforms of the curriculum (ref. 5b). These include vocational and prevocational activities, aimed at disaffected thirteen and fourteen year-olds. These courses, in which the kind of course is determined by pupil choice and available place-ments, cover up to ten hours per week. The general education provided for at least fifteen hours per week is a modified version of the usual curriculum, concentrating on social skills and the basic subjects.

Another example of this genre is the "academy model" (see also further discussion in Chapter IV) (ref. 3c). This is a US high-school programme, effectively a school within a school. It is designed to encourage "at risk" students to complete school (at eighteen in the United States) with marketable skills in a variety of careers. It was started in Philadelphia, in response to concern over high drop-out rates, low achievement and poor work skills in high-school students.

Essentially, a minority of high-school students, specifically those "at risk" of dropping out, but with a commitment to occupational training, are taught together by the same group of teachers. The curriculum includes tutoring in the core subjects of English, maths, science and social studies, as well as some arts, humanities and physical education lessons. Between the ages of fifteen and eighteen, the emphasis on these areas decreases and the emphasis on the vocational lessons grow. Thus in a Business Academy, the curriculum will increasingly include lessons in typing, clerical practice, information processing, office practices and some work experience. Other types of academies will offer curricula in other areas (*e.g.* electronics, horticulture, car mechanics).

The curriculum is enriched in three main ways. Students participate in visits to cultural centres and business organisations in their city. Conversely, members of local businesses visit the academies and talk to the students about their work experiences. Third, students are trained in the skills of job-searching, such as dressing suitably, being interviewed, etc.

This programme depends on a close integration with the local business community in order to make the curriculum as close to a real work experience as possible. This applies even to the extent that work experience is paid.

A programme used in both the United States and Canada, the Teen Outreach Programme (TOP), aims to give point and purpose to aimless lives (ref. 10). The Life Options curriculum is heavily oriented towards social skills. It is taught through small, peer-group meetings, held after school. Pupils are required to take part in community service work.

Like many other programmes it serves pupils from mixed ethnic backgrounds, for about 40 per cent of the TOP students are black, 40 per cent white, 13 per cent Hispanic, and the remainder mostly Native American and Asian. But it was not designed with multi-culturalism in mind. This is a different issue, which is considered in the next section.

The curriculum and multi-culturalism

Many countries report that their "at-risk" groups frequently contain pupils with cultural backgrounds which differ from the majority. This chapter deliberately uses this phrase "pupils with different cultural backgrounds" in preference to "immigrant pupils". Many of the issues which affect the children of immigrants apply just as forcefully to those pupils whose families are indigenous to the country, but who may be denied the privileges and rights accorded to a more powerful culture. In effect, the concerns raised by those whose families have moved in recent generations from one country to another in pursuit of work, or a better life, or security from persecution, serve only to highlight concerns which have always been with us. Few countries are or have ever been the cultural monoliths that stereotype often falsely engenders.

It is often argued that a culturally alien curriculum is one cause of the poor attainment and disaffection felt by some of these pupils. Many countries have experienced pressures to change the cultural content of the curricula followed in their schools, the better to meet the needs of pupils from such minority groups. One of the Canadian case studies specifically refers to the high concentrations of "at risk" students found in minority groups, both in immigrants and in non-English speaking families in Winnipeg (ref. 4a). The Early School Years project, like the Reading/Writing Immersion project mentioned earlier, is specifically designed for these children, and operates at the start of their school career. It aims to provide an enriched language experience so that the project children can better profit from school.

The curriculum component concentrates not just on language development *per se*, but specifically on helping children to use language to learn. Since language is acquired through interaction with others, the opportunity for interaction is increased through employing Language Development Aids. Working with children individually, or in small groups, the adults in the programme (in school, the teachers and the language aids, though parents are also involved in other ways) help to foster such language skills as reporting, logical reasoning, imagining, etc. A training course for participants is an integral part of the programme.

Perhaps the most interesting feature of the case studies of projects involving a high concentration of children from different cultural backgrounds is not what is reported, but what is not reported. All the projects stress the importance of language: few mention the place of the pupil's home or first language, when this is different from the language of instruction used in the school. Most projects aim to help the child gain fluency in the majority language. The place of the child's home language in the school curriculum is rarely considered.

An exception is the Flemish case study, which describes a policy of educational priority with a component for immigrant children that stresses three principles (ref. 11). One of these is respect for the child's own language and culture. Education in the child's own language and culture is a particular feature of the primary curriculum, where up to 50 per cent of the teaching is through the medium of the minority language, provided a set proportion of parents agree.

The question of using a child's home language at school is a difficult one. It is tied up with the complex issue of multi-culturalism. Educationally, it is argued that a smooth introduction to school is more easily achieved when children experience the comfort of the familiar language used at home, at least initially. This helps to avoid alienation. But it also argued that an immersion programme helps to achieve a better mastery of the new language, the one that is essential for educational success, and usually for career prospects later. The debate is also coloured by other issues. In areas when there are many different ethnic minorities, the use of the home language becomes less and less practicable. Thus London schools, with well over a hundred different languages spoken at home, would meet enormous difficulties in finding teaching staff adequately fluent in both English and the minority language. The Flemish report acknowledges this difficulty. But problems in achieving complete linguistic coverage should not prevent the advantages of at least some coverage being thrown away. For some "at risk" children, the start of school can be traumatic enough without having to lose the comfort of one's own language as well.

The school curriculum is only one aspect of policy for helping children from minority cultures, and the question is discussed in depth in the CERI work on cultural and linguistic pluralism (OECD, 1991). This chapter now turns to examine changes in the personnel who help to educate children.

New educators

Everyone is a teacher: from time to time we all help others to learn new skills or to think in different ways. However, we have also created a body of specially-trained people – the teaching profession – so that children, during their formative years at school, can receive learning experiences at the best possible hands.

But have we relied too heavily on the professional competence of the teachers? Is the discontinuity between the sheltered teaching encountered at school and the open learning experiences of real life frustrating? Many children react well to the school cocoon, but perhaps others would profit from a somewhat different experience. Considerations such as these have led some countries to encourage experiments in using people other than teachers to help educate their at-risk children. The most frequently-involved of these "new" educators are the parents.

Parents

The child's first educator is the parent. During the preschool years, when so many social skills are acquired, including the key competence of communicating through speech, it is usually the parent from whom the child mainly learns. The value of encouraging and helping parents of "at risk" children to maintain an involvement and interest in their children's education has been documented by various surveys of compensatory education research. The preceding chapter has discussed their important role in the early years.

There are three main ways in which parents collaborate with the school. One is through school-based social functions, a useful but not novel activity; the second is through taking some responsibility for school planning and policy, discussed later in this chapter; and the third is through an involvement in teaching their children; the subject of this section.

There are many different methods of involving parents in helping to teach their children, ranging from paired reading to the Portage Project (an approach to parental involvement in which a home tutor and parents agree on educational goals for the child that the parents can teach towards at home). These have been well documented in educational literature. Some of the case studies have developed approaches based on these methods. Thus the home learning component of the Early School Years programme in Winnipeg provides support and resources for parents to use with their children (ref. 4*a*). The link between home and school is fostered by a Home Visitor who, on Portage lines, helps parents gain confidence in their role as teacher, enhancing their children's language development in particular.

In the United States, a school following the success for all programmes includes a Family Support Team as part of the project (ref. 3*b*). At one of the project schools this team consisted of "a school social worker, a social worker donated by the Baltimore Department of Social Services, a parent liaison, a part-time counsellor, a part-time nurse practitioner donated by the Maryland Department of Public Health, attendance monitor and a master teacher who works with probationary teachers as well as on staff development". This team meets weekly to review individual problems and to plan parent workshops, aimed at fostering parents' collaboration in their children's education.

A broader strategy was employed by the Partnership in Education project, located in a deprived area of Strathclyde, Scotland (ref. 12). The flavour of this project is best described by a quote:

"All project-based activities focus on parental involvement in the institutions and agencies dealing with the child. This has led to a variety of activities which have been mounted in neighbourhoods, including parent workshops, pre-entrant programmes, parental involvement in class projects, book-based activities, family holidays, drop-in groups, paired reading, play-packs, educational outings, family nights, adult learning opportunities and many, many more."

This project clearly involves parents in many teaching activities, often initiated by requests from parent groups established by the project, rather than led from the school. The purpose of the project is to create and implement ways of forming partnerships in education, so that the parents of young children growing up in a deprived area feel a degree of involvement which would otherwise be missing. The groups, in which parents and professionals meet as equals, are seen in this project as a means to empower parents, so that they can have a strong voice in the education of their children.

In Germany, a report from the Freudenberg Foundation describes the way in which immigrant Turkish mothers have been encouraged to overcome their isolation and to play a part in their children's schooling (ref. 13a). Here, the experience of participating in groups designed initially to help children has also been a catalyst in the mothers' own development, and the project has led to a variety of courses for mothers themselves, an interesting development, which is featured elsewhere, notably in the Canadian case study of the Victor Mager school (ref. 4c).

Virtually all the case studies of primary education projects mention using parents to help educate children. The extent of the involvement is not always described in detail, nor is it always a central thrust of the programme. The case studies noted above are a selection only, intended to illustrate the variety of ideas for involving parents used in projects from different countries. But parents are not the only kind of new educators playing a part in the schools.

Professions other than teaching

Many reports stress that the solution to children "at risk" will not be found through teachers – or any other professions – alone. This is perhaps most obviously recognised by the Belgian report which states: "It is necessary to put in place a policy from which no innovator is to be excluded".

The reports goes on to list a multi-disciplinary network of individuals, such as psychologists, medical doctors, educationalists and social workers as well as organisations contributing to the developments described (ref. 14).

The Australian contribution, to which we revert later, describes a mechanism for integrating health, education and welfare services and professionals dealing with pupils with serious social and behavioural difficulties (ref. 15*b*).

At the level of the individual pupil and school, the contribution of the educational or school psychologist is well known, and most projects do not dwell on this. Several case studies offer descriptions of developments involving social workers in school. In Germany, where school-based social work is policy in some *Länder*, the social worker and youth welfare worker play a part in the school-to-work transition, discussed in the next chapter.

Other case studies have used social workers more directly as educators. One report describes vividly how school-based social workers can intervene to facilitate the education of socially-disadvantaged children at secondary school (ref. 13*b*). In this scheme, the Weinheim comprehensive school developed the idea of the "All-day School", later modified to a "Pupils' Support Group". This was originally run by two school social workers, with help from some of the teaching staff. Some of the pupils in the Support Group are immigrants, others come from stressful family situations, yet others are "at risk" of addiction, or delinquents, or with serious learning difficulties: they attend school, but few attend lessons on a regular basis.

The Support Group offers rooms, materials and other resources for a rich menu of activities which the pupils themselves organise. Some, such as the development of a pupils' workshop, enable pupils to develop and acquire skills which relate to real-life situations. Others involve projects which are remote from the traditional curriculum – one example is how the gift of an old billiard table led to the establishment of a thriving billiards club. What these support activities do is to change pupils' attitudes towards school, to enable pupils to see school as a centre of interesting and enhancing pursuits, and to foster an understanding of the personal rewards gained through making a contribution to the community.

One of the interesting aspects of the Weinheim case study is the collaboration between teachers and social workers in the education of young people. Another is the continuing participation of former members of the Support Group, who act as project helpers, group leaders, committee members, etc. Some of these former pupils are unemployed; others are now students, trainees, and skilled workers. Their contribution is an example of the community at large acting as educators, a theme taken up in several case studies and a theme which we now examine.

The community

A separate section on the role of community members as educators is, in one sense, unnecessary. The teachers, parents, social workers and others mentioned in the preceding paragraphs are all members of that amorphous body, the community, and the school itself is an institution set in the community. In today's more open society the community has access to many hitherto well-guarded preserves, from government departments to hospitals, and traditionalists in education cannot expect to prevent community access to schools. What distinguishes some of these case studies of educational innovation is not access itself, but extent – the extent to which others in the community play a part in the task of educating, and the extent to which schools encourage and exploit this in the interests of "at risk" children.

The Weinheim School Support Group builds on the support of many organisations in order to offer pupils the chance of participating in such diverse educational activities as a choir, body-building, basketball, etc. For example, an international basketball camp, organised by the Group, was supported by the forestry department, the municipal culture department, the youth welfare department, the fire brigade, the Red Cross, the armed forces, political parties, churches, local industries and other bodies. This was a particularly ambitious project: but it illustrates how, given leadership, a network of different organisations can collaborate in giving meaning and purpose to the school experience of children "at risk".

The Victor Mager school, in Winnipeg, Canada, serves an area with high concentrations of low-income families, high unemployment, single parents, parents with low educational achievement, and immigrant families (ref. 4c). As well as seeking to work with community organisations, the school programme particularly emphasises the role of individuals in the life of the school. Approximately fifty volunteers participate in a variety of ways in school, providing additional assistance for students and staff. The school employs a "volunteer co-ordinator", whose job is to assess volunteer needs, provide such training as volunteers may need and to supervise and support their activities. The co-ordinator also actively recruits volunteers, often deliberately seeking support from families with low educational achievement, who need encouragement to offer their help.

In the US report, the Academy Model schools depend on community involvement (ref. 3c). In this case, however, the involvement is clearly focused on one section of the community – the business or industrial community, depending on the curriculum bias of the individual academy. The work-experience part of the programme could not take part without local industry contributing time, interest and facilities to the pupils' education. The report does point out that this kind of community contribution is not always easy to obtain, particularly at a time of recession, for when the local employment situation deteriorates, industry has to cut its costs, and placement becomes harder to find.

Community involvement is not just local persons and institutions offering service to the school. It is a two-way street, for the school itself can offer service to the community, another valuable educational experience for pupils. Quite apart from the social gains, community service sometimes shades into vocational experience. The Teen Outreach Programme is an illustration of community service planned, where possible, to match pupils' vocational interests.

Where people make an input, they often want a voice. As parents and community organisations contribute to the curriculum, the next step is to give them a say in shaping the curriculum and in deciding policy. In the Academy Model (e.g. Stern, Raby and Dayton, 1992) the business community plays a part through an Advisory Board, which manages the programme. This is a very different situation from that traditional view of school management, in which the school is seen as an organisation run by a head teacher in the same individual way as a sea-captain runs a ship. This leads us to consider the changed systems of managing schools deployed in so many of the case studies.

Shared responsibilities

A school is an activity in which there are no spectators: all are players – the head teacher, the teachers, the parents, the employers, both local and national, and the pupils. In many traditional systems, major decisions about equipment, playing roles, even the leagues and competitions to enter, are made by outside bodies. One of the features of these case studies is the emphasis placed on reducing the influence of these outside bodies – the district board, or local education authority – and encouraging more of the players to take responsibility for the play. The first to consider are parents and others, particularly employers.

Parents and others

Parents are often mentioned as key personnel. The Australian contribution describes parent participation as a criterion of good practice for programmes associated with children "at risk", from either the primary or secondary school level (ref. 15*a*). Participation, in this view, includes involving parents in decision-making about policies in a shared, negotiated process with staff and students through membership of the school council or subcommittees such as finance or curriculum.

Similar sentiments are expressed in the philosophy underlying the Accelerated Schools Model, established in the United States, which refers to the importance of providing an expanded role in school governance for all key participants, including, among others, parents (ref. 3*d*). Parents sit on the "cadres", small subcommittees dealing with specific issues, on the steering committee which co-ordinates and organises the "cadres", and attend the "school-as-a-whole" meetings.

The case study of Jefferson school, San Francisco, reports that the introduction of the Accelerated Schools Model has substantially increased parental involvement. But the same case study also points out that this school departs from the intended project structure, in that parents rarely attend "cadre" meetings, and that major decisions are not taken at "school-as-a-whole" meetings, but at bi-weekly meetings of the principal and school staff.

In Madison elementary school, Missouri, the other case study school on this programme, the "cadres" are largely composed of faculty members, with one parent representative. There is also a single parent representative (who rarely attends) on the steering committee. The overview of these two schools, while making a number of positive comments, noted that these two schools failed to empower parents significantly.

The Comer Process aims to help disadvantaged children succeed at school through revitalising bonds between school, family and community (ref. 3*e*). A parent programme is concerned with social activities. In Comer schools the School Planning and Management Team is described as the backbone without which the programme cannot be implemented. But this Team, which is the governing body in a Comer Process school, contains only a single parent representative. The case studies of the Comer Process schools do show parents being involved successfully in school governance. However, school staff do not believe that they have achieved as much parent participation as they would have liked.

The teachers

Immured within the four walls of her classroom, the teacher in the traditional school was given little scope for development outside of immediate classroom issues. Her decisions were classroom decisions, limited to the lessons and the pupils she taught. Wider issues, affecting the life of the school where she worked and the content of the curriculum she taught were generally the concerns of others, sometimes close by, but often remote and sometimes inaccessible.

In changing the school's relationships with the community it serves, parental empowerment, as described above, is important. But these changes in role and relationship and – even more directly – the changes in the curriculum described earlier, centrally involve the school staff, including the principal. Their practices, often of long standing, have to be modified. Their support is needed if these changes are to be effective: how has this support been achieved?

Case studies from the United States, the United Kingdom and Italy developed this approach. The US contribution includes some case studies of radical changes in the place of teachers in school governance. Three programmes are particularly relevant, the Comer Process, the "School-Based Management" programme and the "Success for All" programme (ref. 3b, 3e, 3f).

In a Comer Process school, one central principle is that decisions should be the result of consensus. This principle is actioned by a School Planning and Management Team (SPMT), composed of the principal, representatives of the teachers, a parent representative and representatives of ancillary staff. But power nevertheless resides with the principal, who holds a veto. In the case study of the Comer Process schools in New Haven, Connecticut, the veto has been removed, and decisions are now taken by majority vote.

The SPMTs are seen as the backbone of the Comer Process. To quote a principal's comments, "Everything goes through the SPMT (...). We write a school plan every spring, based on our problems and needs, and we actually work through it. Teachers are obligated to follow the school plan in their lesson plans. People who have had a say in the process are more likely to follow that process".

The case studies do not provide details of the weighting of the different constituencies represented on the SPMT, nor of the method of choosing teacher representatives (election? selection? sub-group representation? etc.) But the principle is clear: teamwork and collaboration among teaching staff and between teaching staff and others is seen as one of the keys to the successful operation of schools serving children "at risk". The US report speaks very highly of the Comer Process approach. Commenting on the New Haven experiment, it writes: "One of the most noted accomplishments (...) (of the Comer Process) is the stunning success of the two original schools: they went from ranking among the worst in the district to among the best in the areas of student achievement, attendance, and behaviour".

This view appears to depend on the amount of latitude that schools are given by higher authority. In the second Comer Process case study, Prince George's County, Maryland, the Comer Process was instituted by the district as a result of a court order to reorganise schools. Here the superintendent retains strong central control, and schools have little opportunity to influence major issues, such as the content of the curriculum. The SPMTs role is largely that of planning activities, leading to a teacher's comment that "The SPMT is an advisory (body). I don't believe Prince George's County is going to let teachers make decisions, much less parents".

The School-Based Management (SBM) case studies attempt to avoid any possible resentment and resistance to reforms instituted from "on high" by placing responsibility for reform unambiguously on the teachers' shoulders. Conversely, the role of the principal is diminished. In Dade County, Miami, proposals for changing the governance structure of the schools along SBM lines must be submitted with the approval of two-thirds of the staff. If the plan is approved by the existing school board and district, principals are allocated a seat (with one vote) on the school's new decision making "cadre" (committee).

In Juarez school, Sante Fe, teachers drafted a proposal to replace the position of principal with a management team of four teachers, elected by their colleagues. The proposal was accepted by the school board.

In the Success for All programme, essentially based on curriculum change, and requiring a substantial financial commitment, the principal has to demonstrate the approval of at least 75 per cent of the classroom teachers before the programme can be introduced.

These new ways of managing schools seek to achieve a united approach, a consistent school ethos. To this extent the philosophy resonates with the "whole-school approach" to children with special needs. The secretaries, classroom assistants, school caretaker, etc., have important parts to play in achieving this, recognised in some of the case studies by the place allocated to them on decision-making bodies. In line with the metaphor at the start of this section, they too are players, adults with a different relationship with children from that of the teachers. These relationships can be very significant to children "at risk", where relationships with parents may be damaged and fraught.

Four case studies of secondary schools in the United Kingdom, all of which had a large proportion of "at risk" pupils on roll, describe whole school approaches through different methods (ref. 18). One school emphasised the quality of relationships between teachers and pupils; a second used an assessment procedure, "records of achievement", which give pupils a substantial part in the assessment procedure as a way of integrating assessment into the curriculum; a third school developed a method of "reflective dialogue" to improve relationships and control behaviour difficulties. This approach was designed to develop confidence and also to create responsibility in the pupils for their own learning. This school noted marked improvements in examination results and particular success in a national competition.

In the fourth school, emphasis was placed on the professional commitment of teachers and the development of school ethos. The school set about analysing its own strengths and weaknesses, a process which led to a school values statement.

These approaches all involved head teachers in creating with and through the staff, new whole school approaches aimed at raising standards, confidence, teaching skills, etc. Qualitative evaluations were carried out and the report describes success, although to varying degrees, in all schools.

In Italy, case studies of particularly depressed regions of Palermo in Sicily reported whole school ecosystem approaches which involved pupils, teachers and parents in improving the attainments of "at risk" pupils (ref. 19). Professionals – e.g. head teachers, teachers and educational psychologists work together in schools and with families via discussion groups, seminars and training sessions to develop intervention plans, school-family relationships and communication between services.

Evaluations revealed initially encouraging results, with improvements shown on a number of cognitive and reading tests at both primary and intermediate levels.

This ecosystem concept also promotes the "quartier", and gives residents pride and a reason for staying there. The programme stresses the value and importance of education, and aims to create a climate of opinion which is hostile to truancy and drop-out.

Supporters of these "whole-school" approaches see initial and in-service teacher training as key features in their programmes. They find that the experience of working in the programme can often be itself an effective training.

Resources and reorganisation

Introducing new curricula and drawing on new educators entails changes in the way schools operate. Two particular questions emerge. How are these changes funded? How much autonomy do schools have for these purposes?

Funding methods

To change a system usually requires funding – either money or resources in-kind. Many of the case studies refer to the appointment of additional personnel, both teachers and others. Many mention a reduced teaching load for teachers carrying different responsibilities, which implies the appointment of extra teaching staff, even if this is not stated in the report. Some projects, such as the Success for All programme described above, have also engaged the time of a variety of other professionals.

Extra funding for experimental programmes, limited to a small number of schools raises few problems. Several of the innovations described in the case studies are partially or totally funded by charitable foundations. But no charity is likely to be rich enough to fund a significant programme for all a country's schools.

When a programme is introduced nationally, it requires central funding. Equitable principles for allocating funds have to be established. One such principle uses the characteristics of an area – its unemployment figures, social security payments, delinquency data, for example, to come to a judgement to increase resources to all its schools. The Zones of Educational Priority (ZEP), described in a French case study, are illustrations of this principle. ZEP are usually designated to overlap with areas which are already receiving priority assistance for urban renewal and social support. Schools within the ZEP receive extra teaching posts and operating subsidies.

Another clear description of fine-tuning resource allocation is provided by the Netherlands programme. In this programme, the school, not the area, is the basis for funding at the primary level. Resources are allocated to individual primary schools according to the characteristics of the children and their families. Each pupil is given a specific weighting, depending on the education, occupation and ethnicity of the parent(s). The schools are allocated teachers in proportion to their weighted pupil numbers. (Secondary schools are allocated extra resources only when they have pupils from ethnic minority backgrounds.)

The Netherlands case study also illustrates a different funding principle, the use of monies from sources other than education. The second arm of its Educational Priority Policy is the Educational Priority Area Policy. Here, schools with a high proportion of disadvantaged pupils are members of a network of different organisations located in nationally-recognised educational priority areas. The network offers opportunities for schools to participate in joint activities with local organisations such as libraries, community centres, etc. These joint activities illustrate the place of community organisations in the education of children "at risk", described in the preceding section. The point here is that funding for the activities comes partly from non-educational sources, in this particular case the Ministry of Welfare, Health and Social Affairs.

This highlights the view that children "at risk" are at risk outside school as well as in it. Important though school is, and notwithstanding the central part that it plays – or should play – in young people's lives, other organisations, too, have a part to play in combating disadvantage. The Netherlands report demonstrates the use of additional (not alternative) sources of finance for those activities which are as much social as educational. Co-operative funding enables joint programmes to be developed.

Autonomy

Schools with high proportions of "at risk" children are themselves at risk of low morale and poor image. Where standards of attainment are depressed, staff and pupils alike are in danger of feeling failures. Commitment is lacking.

Several case studies use the argument that one way to improve commitment and to give back to school staffs a feeling of involvement, is to increase their personal responsibility for management of the school's resources. This means that many of the decisions which might have been taken by administrators at local level are now taken at school level. The extent of this empowerment of the school varies. It might mean only that the school is encouraged to use extra resources for "at risk" children as it wishes. Or the school might be given a fixed budget for all its teaching equipment and materials, which it can use as it wishes. Or it might mean that the school is given a budget to cover all its activities, not merely the purchase of teaching equipment, but such matters as the maintenance and development of buildings and land, and the hiring of staff and payment of their salaries. However far this autonomy extends, the principle is the same: greater devolution of decision-making to the point where the decision is felt; greater empowerment of the individual school and its management structure – a central feature of educational reforms in the United Kingdom.

Examples of devolution are furnished by some of the US case studies. In the "School-based Management" initiatives, school principals are given enhanced authority over the school's budget (ref. 3*f*). In the Dade County, Florida, scheme, the school budget is allocated to the school council of each participating school as a lump sum payment. Spending priorities, staff-hiring, and other administrative tasks are then determined by the school council. As a result of this policy, schools with special or "at risk" populations have often established new programmes to meet these needs. These are policies they have themselves developed, not policies imposed from elsewhere.

Juarez elementary school, Santa Fe, New Mexico, is another example of "School-based Management". This school serves approximately 700 "highly-transient" students, of whom three-quarters receive assistance with lunch costs, and two-thirds are Hispanic. In the Santa Fe school district, staff are not responsible for the development of the school budget. But this school participates in the Schools Improvement Programme, which offers funding (provided by the Panasonic Foundation) for teacher-initiated reforms. In order to gain funding, these reforms have to spring from teachers, not school principals, reflecting the belief that effective reform begins in the classroom. In addition, the programme provides consultancy on restructuring school organisation and on grant opportunities. As a result of these activities, Juarez school has been enabled to operate a summer school, employ a school psychologist, support staff attendance at conferences and offer parent-education classes. The case study reported the tremendous pride the students showed in their school.

As noted earlier, legislation has been introduced in the United Kingdom to enable schools to control their own budgets in this way. This principle of Local Management of Schools was first applied to larger secondary schools, but has since been extended to include both primary and special schools. It is therefore an attempt to influence the whole education system, and not just that part of it which is concerned with children "at risk".

So far this chapter has concentrated on analysing and describing the principles and practices which characterise the case studies. We now turn to examine the messages that the case studies send.

Signals from the case studies

The relevance of the case studies

The material presented in this chapter is based on descriptions of major projects, usually illustrated with case studies of individual schools. The chosen schools have, understandably, served depressed, impoverished areas. The descriptions of the school populations refer without exception to the high incidences of unemployment, of single-parent families, of ethnic minorities, of transient families – the pupils are indeed "at risk" in the sense of this report. They showed the poor attainments, low attendance figures and severe behaviour problems that illustrated their alienation from the education offered. Yet many schools in favoured locations would be proud of the school atmosphere, the teacher morale, the pupils' attainment and behaviour that many of these schools are now reported to have achieved as a result of the activities described in the case studies. In short, the changes and reforms reported have a wider educational relevance than their immediate context would suggest: what is good for children "at risk" may be good for all children.

How easy is curriculum reform?

But the reforms described in the earlier part of this chapter are not introduced effortlessly, though some efforts are less demanding than others. Changing the curriculum to meet the different needs of the "at risk" population is felt by many contributors to be less difficult to implement than other innovations. An example is paying more and better attention to the reading and language elements in the curriculum of the primary school.

This is a well-tried nostrum for children with learning difficulties. The point to note from these case studies is the extent to which the programmes have swung from remediation to prevention. No case study features a programme directed primarily at seven and eight year olds: programmes are focused on children starting school and in some cases at preschool children.

Even here there are tensions which the project reports do not always bring out. A reading and language curriculum which more effectively reflects minority culture may not be easy to implement in a school where several different cultures meet. On the other hand, an effort to pursue recognising minority interests, exemplified by the "Multicultural Advisory Committee" set up as part of the comprehensive programme at Victor Mager school in Winnipeg undoubtedly helps (ref. 4c).

Introducing a new curriculum is more difficult. An example is a curriculum which captures the vocational interests of young people, often cited as a successful reform at the secondary stage. Where countries have laid down a national curriculum which all pupils have to follow, this must be sufficiently flexible to accommodate such a scheme. The programme may require teachers with different competencies. It will require bridges to be built with local industry. It is not always easy for schools to put such a curriculum in place alongside an existing orthodox one. Where these practical difficulties have been overcome, as in the "school within a school" idea (ref. 3c), the reports are positive.

The place of parents

With few exceptions, all the projects stress the importance of gaining parental support. Parental support for and involvement in social activities, such as fund-raising, is a feature common to many projects. Projects also succeed in encouraging parents to help in educating their children, particularly young children. But involving parents in the governance of the school is much more difficult, even though this is seen as a key element in many of the reforms.

All parents lead busy lives outside school, and arrangements for encouraging participation in school governance have to cater to this. For example, committee meetings may have to be held well outside normal school hours. Parents of children "at risk" may be doubly disenfranchised. The poor, possibly without such facilities as personal transport, telephone, etc., will find committee membership difficult to sustain. In addition, their attitude to school may not be positive. They themselves often do not possess a history of school success, and their memories of school may be unhappy, coloured by long-term failure.

It requires a particular effort to encourage such parents into realising that their opinion is important and can have a significant effect on the education provided for their children. So some programmes have gone out of their way to build bridges with parents in ways not usually considered part of a school's responsibility. The Victor Mager school in Winnipeg has set up a combined academic/job training programme for single mothers (ref. 4c). The group formed for the "Turkish Children and Mother" project at Gelsenkirchen, Germany, has as one of its objectives the promotion of opportunities for further education of family members, particularly women (ref. 13a). Although it might be reasonable to hope that providing support of such clear relevance to the lives of deprived families would encourage the growth of a group of parents who would in return be willing to contribute a parental input to the school's governance, this is not mentioned by these projects.

Even the one project which specifically focuses on empowering parents, the "Partnership in Education" project in Strathclyde, has of yet nothing to say on this issue (ref. 12). That last "yet" is added deliberately; changing the attitudes of parents in deprived areas to such an extent that they feel confident to take decisions alongside professionals may well prove to be a long-term process. We may have to wait for a generation before we see parents come forward in large numbers to take their places on school boards and governing bodies. Even then, the difficult question of incentives, or at least some compensation for time given, may have to be addressed. One such incentive, not discussed in the projects, is training for parents in the responsibilities attached to membership of governing bodies.

The community

Few case studies mention difficulties in gaining and retaining the support of local community institutions, whether this is given on the grounds of community spirit or of enlightened self-interest. An exception occurs in several secondary school projects, which had introduced vocational courses with work placements arranged through local employers. At times of recession, such placements become hard to obtain. But even where support is freely available, some time and effort is required from the school in negotiating this. This raises the substantial issue of the role of the school teaching staff.

The school staff

The changes in the role of the parents and local institutions reflect changes based on the philosophy of reforming schools through returning them to the democratic control of their communities. But these also involve change in the role of the teachers. Case studies, to varying degrees, see the empowerment of parents and local institutions going hand in hand with the empowerment of the teacher – the classroom teacher. Successful projects refer to the presence of teacher representatives in all the influential bodies in the school's governance structure. This has considerable implications for the role of the principal, or headteacher, who has to move from being, as is currently the case in some educational systems, "captain of the ship" to "chairman of the board", stripped of much power. Indeed, as mentioned above, in one of the case studies from the United States, the staff abolished the position of the principal, replacing it with an elected four-person collective (ref. 3f). In another US case study of the same programme, principals were compensated for this alteration in their responsibilities by increasing their salaries. The implications that this issue, the effects that movements to democratise the school staff have on the role of principal, needs careful consideration in the light of the school's management structure and career opportunities in the teaching profession.

The change in the role of the teacher attracts more comment. Reports state that giving teachers more direct responsibility for the life of the school increases their sense of professionalism, and improves morale. Schools become better places, but at a price. The obvious price is paid in teachers' time. Governing a school democratically, opening it out to the community, even affecting a small change in the curriculum involves time. Projects have dealt with this in different ways.

Changes occur not only in the teachers' managerial role, but also in their relation to the curriculum. As teachers are given greater freedom to modify curricula to meet the needs of individual pupils, so do their images more closely match the perception of "autonomous professionals".

The teachers at the four Manitoba inner-city schools introducing the Reading/Writing Immersion project not only met a half to a full day each week for ten months prior to introducing the programme, they also met for one full day each month during the programme's operation (ref. 4b). The Lisbon teachers were given time for meetings for curriculum development (ref. 5a). At the Weinheim comprehensive school, teachers contributing regularly to the Pupils' Support Group network were given up to five hours per week time credit (ref. 13b). Time was also granted to teachers in Italy to develop the ecosystem approaches described there (ref. 19). The point is not discussed in the United Kingdom report where the new approaches were probably developed as part of the general management plans of the schools.

A different incentive from "time in lieu" is the provision of extra staff, not to relieve the teachers but to support them. This can be additional, not alternative. Thus the Lisbon programme appointed teacher-counsellors to lead the curriculum development meetings mentioned above, and to support the teachers in the classroom.

The pilot school for the "Success for All" programme appointed an additional six tutors, an extra teacher (to reduce class size), an extra preschool teacher and an aide, an extended day kindergarten teacher and aides, and a social worker (ref. 3b). Where the Comer Process was introduced, ''Facilitators'' were appointed to help the schools adjust to the new way of working. But as both these programmes were extended to other schools, funding limitations resulted in less support. The report (ref. 3e) states baldly that ''resource constraints are a major determinant of success''.

It is worth noting, however, that the main resource input was needed when a school first introduced the Comer Process programme: as the programme proceeded, teachers became more comfortable with their new roles and required less support. In theory, as schools gained autonomy and manage their own affairs, there should be a trade-off: the number of staff required at district or area level should decrease as schools assume more of the responsibilities previously handled elsewhere. This point is not mentioned: its impact is probably not large.

Few case studies give the direct cost of these improved services. An exception is one of the curriculum-based projects, the Comprehensive Competency Programme, which quotes an average cost of $12.46 per instructional hour (ref. 8a). The costing assumptions would need to be examined in order to determine the meaning of that figure.

Autonomy

The idea of a self-governing, self-managing school has attractions, for projects speak warmly of the motivation gained from giving schools more autonomy. But these are reports of individual projects, not of country-wide education services.

In fact the two concepts, autonomous schools on the one hand and an education service on the other are in opposition to one another. To illustrate this, there are issues for which co-ordination at area or even national level is needed. Good provision for pupils with special needs is an example. High quality facilities might be another. A structure with some powers over individual schools is needed to achieve this. In short, the question is not whether to give autonomy to individual schools or not, but rather how much and what kind of autonomy to give in regard to which aspects of educational decision-making and with what degrees of constraint.

Effective change requires training

In the programmes emphasising changes in school management and governance, the teacher's role is redefined. In contrast to many existing systems, where teachers teach and principals manage, teachers have to learn some of the skills of management. They have to be familiar with the techniques of person-management, of budgeting, of interviewing, etc. The psychological prize of motivation through involvement is gained at the expense of specialisation. There is little questioning of the wisdom of this bargain, for the case studies agree that the prize is great. But there is an obvious need for training teachers in these new roles and, almost without exception, the case studies dealing with new approaches to school governance stress this – as too do those dealing with curriculum change.

The Reading Recovery programme is essentially a technique for teaching effective reading strategies. It is thus hardly a radical curriculum reform, nor does it require a change in teacher role. Yet even here the report of its introduction states categorically "the training model is the foundation of the programme". This is a two-stage model. First, teacher leaders are trained through a year's full-time course. They then pass on their skills to those teachers who will follow the programme in their schools. This second stage training includes attending a class on one night a week during a training year, and some five sessions a year thereafter.

The lesson is clear. If more substantial reforms involving new curricula are to be successful, a commensurately more thorough preparation and training programme ought to be instituted. This point applies with equal force when teachers carry new roles, as in some of the school-based management programmes.

These issues relate to the in-service education and training of serving teachers. There is no case study of a project monitoring the value of changes in initial training procedures. Yet in any major change in an education service, initial and in-service training go hand in hand. Where changes in the education of "at risk" children are contemplated, initial training ought not to be forgotten.

Pastoral care

One particular theme from virtually all the case studies well deserves reiteration, *i.e.* it would be foolhardy to imagine that education alone can cure the ills of deprivation. As the school emerges into the community, collaboration with other professions and other organisations is seen as a key feature by many programmes.

The Belgian case study offers a description of a network of linkages, to illustrate the multi-disciplinary nature of the various ongoing activities (ref. 14). One such activity, described in several projects, is the pastoral care of the individual pupil.

Here two different approaches have been illustrated. One is school-based, as in some of the United States programmes. In the Comer Process, when resources permit, each school establishes a mental health team, composed of teachers, administrators, social workers, psychologists and nurses (ref. 3e). In the United Kingdom report (ref. 18) positive approaches by all teachers are seen as an essential component to developing good attitudes and behaviour.

The other approach relies on facilities based outside the school as in the Interagency Referral Process. In this Australian scheme, health, education and welfare services are induced to co-operate in the interest of individual pupils "at risk".

Both approaches have their advantages. The school-based team must deal with more pupils, but at school level initially. The Interagency Team, like a child guidance service, probably deals with fewer pupils, but has an immediate access to area-based resources. The two different contributions are probably best seen as complementary, for both rest on the principle of harnessing inter-professional co-operation and can deal constructively with a continuum of difficulty.

The place of pupils

Many of the case studies emphasise the idea of empowerment. The teachers, the parents, community leaders – in the new schools described in these reports, these are the people to whom power to effect change is given. The place of one centrally-concerned group of people is rarely discussed – the pupils themselves. Yet they are in every sense the key participants. It is to them that this educational endeavour is directed; it is their disaffection with their educational experience that is the heart of the matter. Some countries do mention this. Thus an Australian report states that the criteria for judging the success of programmes for children and young people "at risk" include "strategies to empower students (...)" (ref. 15a).

This view is of more significance for older, more mature pupils, particularly at the secondary stage of education. In one of the United Kingdom studies, involving pupils in the assessment procedures was seen as an important way of developing confidence. The case study of the Weinheim school in Germany discussed empowerment in a broad context (ref. 13b).

"The active aspect (...) (of the Pupils' Support Group, which sets up both school activities and leisure activities) is provided by the pupils themselves, with the content reflecting the actual needs of the young people involved."

Although the report points out that the ideas mainly originate from sources outside the school, it goes on to state:

"In the case of options planned on a long-term basis it is increasingly the young people themselves who are responsible for organisation and administration."

This approach to empowering pupils can be contrasted with another case study of a successful innovation, the Academy model, from the United States (ref. 3c). Here the report speaks of Academy teachers believing that traditional methods of direct instruction help meet their students' need for structure:

"They need to be spoon-fed and the Academy makes that possible."

Clearly there are very different views on the place of pupils. This may reflect innovations stemming from the different traditions and different cultures. Even within the same country, what suits one context may not suit another. It is a pity that substantial discussion of the role of pupils, was largely absent from the case studies.

The time scale

One other quite different feature is common to most of the case studies. The descriptions are all of activities and re-organisations that have taken time to initiate and time to appraise. The Australian Interagency Referral Process was one result of a 1988 report to the South Australian Government (ref. 15b). The programme was established in 1990. The report to the OECD, though positive in tone and recommending the replication of the programme to other countries, is at pains to point out that these are provisional conclusions, resting on an ongoing evaluation, which has yet to be completed.

This illustrates the three elements in the time question. First, time is needed to prepare and plan the innovation. Those to be involved have to be given time to discuss, to accept and to support changes, sometimes very substantial changes, in their work and lives. The case studies stress the need to persuade teachers in particular, for they may have to change both what they teach and how they work. Some programmes state that a strong majority of the teaching staff must actively desire the change as a precondition of its introduction. Change cannot be imposed:

"A man convinced against his will is of the same opinion still."

Teaching is in many countries a highly-unionised profession. Some of the US programmes pay specific attention to the importance of union support. Thus in both case studies of the School-Based Management programme, mention is made of union support for the innovations, and in one case, union concessions (ref. 3*f*). Again, these negotiations require time.

Second, time is needed for the innovation to have effect. Participants have to adjust to new conditions. A new curriculum needs time to bed down. Sudden, dramatic improvements in such characteristics as the behaviour, attainment and attendance of "at risk" pupils cannot be expected. The case studies work to time scales not of months but years.

Only then can the third phase, the final evaluation, be made. This is not to say that on-going formative evaluations of projects are not needed: on the contrary, they are a useful and valuable feature of the reports. But the early stages of an innovation may be affected by "running-in" problems. Alternatively, some projects report that early stages are coloured by an enthusiasm which wanes as the programme proceeds.

Both these points are arguments for delaying thoughtful, considered evaluation until some time has passed. They are also used to argue for a step-by-step introduction of programme features. No one wants several "running-in" problems to occur simultaneously, for the burden of coping may become too heavy. Moreover, if enthusiasm wanes over time, there are positive advantages in a stepwise introduction, for this avoids the possibility of the programme going on the back-burner after initial publicity has ceased. This emphasis on gradual change will still further increase the time span of successful change.

Closing comment

The school changes described in these case studies illustrate how to offer a more rewarding experience to deprived children and youth. Their effects constitute a great prize – school-leavers entering the community with better skills and more positive attitudes. The changes are essential for "at risk" children; they are probably valuable for all children.

That the examples summarised in this chapter contain lessons that are relevant to all children should not be surprising. After all, those "at risk" are not members of a different category of human being and there is no reason why effective educational methods for CYAR should be qualitatively different from those that work with other children. As indicated in the first chapter of this report the concept of ''at risk'' is an optimistic one if it is interpreted preventively. For prevention to work it means that those who would otherwise have been ''at risk'' will now be able to function well in ordinary educational circumstances. For this reason alone it is preferable that teaching methods developed for those ''at risk'' as well as those who are not ''at risk'' have much in common.

The disappointments with education that were outlined at the start of this chapter can and should be made to disappear, and a belief in the value of school restored. To borrow a misrendering of Helvetius's maxim, *l'éducation peut tout*: if education cannot achieve everything, there is hardly anything it cannot achieve.

Conclusions

Although children are ''at risk'' for many different reasons and although they are to be found in many different situations, rural as well as urban, these case studies demonstrate that the highest concentrations of need, the most urgent problems, exist in the rundown, deprived areas of the inner city. Some of the disheartening descriptions of the populations served by these schools make moving reading. Small wonder that the quality of life – or existence – there, leads to bitterness and anger.

Yet there are some glimpses of hope. When the resentment of the inner city spills over into riot, it is rarely the schools that are torched. The education service offers help to many families, help that is constant and practical, not capricious and palliative. School does offer a way to reach alienated communities. Parents neither want to damage opportunities for their children, nor do they want to reject the chance of improving these, however negatively they may feel about other initiatives. So these innovations are important, not solely for the educational improvements they offer, but also for the influence they may bring to bear on wider social and economic problems.

Keypoints

The simplest innovations increase the emphasis on language skills at the start of school

For those wishing to implement change, the easiest measures to introduce are probably those that are centred on the curriculum. Of the different measures described, the simplest and thus probably the least expensive (but not inexpensive), are changes in the primary curriculum. Here, the programmes described are usually changes of emphasis, concentrating on raising standards, particularly in language skills and reading. In some ways these changes are the direct descendants of the remedial and compensatory programmes of earlier decades. They are aimed at the very first years in school. At their simplest, they are school-based, and even parents are only peripherally involved. More complex programmes combine school tuition with planned parent participation. This kind of parental support is not difficult to gain, even in deprived areas. There is little dependable evidence on the long-term effect of these programmes, though short-term effects are clearly positive.

New secondary curricula, stressing prevocational and vocational courses are effective, but can be complex to organise

Curriculum change at the secondary level is described in some studies. This is probably more difficult to effect, for it usually involves introducing quite new courses. The examples given often have some links with business and industry. They require a flexible school organisation to operate successfully. Moreover, in countries with centrally determined curricula, their content may well be at variance with national requirements, unless these are designed to permit and accommodate exceptions. They have little parental teaching input designed, though this may occur adventitiously.

Comprehensive reformation of school government and management offers great reward, but is a difficult and delicate task, requiring capable long-term leadership

Some of the programmes intended to improve education through reforming school government and management have had marked success. They are probably more difficult still to introduce effectively, for they can involve substantial changes in the roles of all the players. Broadly, senior members of the current hierarchy, head-teachers and district officials, lose power: junior members, classroom teachers and parents, gain it. It can be no bad thing for democracies to democratise education: but just as a movement from an authoritarian to a democratic system is difficult and dangerous at the level of the state, so is it at the level of the school. It needs planning, leadership, and it takes time.

Joint programmes, supported by the combined efforts of departments of education, social work and employment in particular, should have much to offer the school

Many programmes mention collaboration between educators and other professions, for the problems of children "at risk" will not be solved by the education service alone. Collaboration is easy to preach, difficult to practice: different professions march to different music. Collaboration between members of two different professions is probably more effective when one agency is responsible for both, and when there is a single chain of command. While there are examples of collaboration at the school level, there are few persuasive examples of effective interdepartmental collaboration at government level. Yet this is where the example should be set.

The two key features of successful innovations are time and training for teachers

Nearly all the programmes, whether concerned with curriculum or governance, mention training for the teachers involved. In successful programmes, this is not a haphazard affair. It starts before the innovation starts, and often continues throughout the introduction of the programme. Its importance cannot be underestimated. It is probably one of the two most powerful incentives in encouraging teachers to bite the bullet of change. The other is time. Of all the resources that teachers seek in introducing these innovations, time is the most often mentioned. It is a tribute to the altruism of the teaching profession that these two issues, time and training, are given greater emphasis than salary increases. Any country seeking to transform its schools must be sensitive to these two points above all others.

Special efforts are needed to help parents overcome their reluctance to participate in school governance

Many programmes stress the importance of giving parents a strong voice in managing the new schools. Case studies often report difficulties in implementing this, in contrast to the relative willingness of parents to help with the education of young children. Where success has been claimed, it has had to be worked for, often through a long period of trust-building, starting early. Parents of "at risk" children often have to be encouraged into partnership and may want preparation for this. They have particular practical difficulties to overcome: incentives should help.

School reform cannot be accomplished cheaply: apart from time and training, other costs have to be recognised and met

These points raise issues of funding and resources. Programmes report that offering schools greater control over their own resources is a valuable stimulus to change. Autonomy alone is not the answer. All projects involve extra funding of some kind: reform cannot be achieved cheaply. Teachers may be willing to give a little time, but successful programmes do not attempt to exploit their professionalism and have provided extra staff to compensate for extra demands. These and other costs are sometimes provided centrally, sometimes through charitable foundations. More funds are needed at the start of a programme than later.

In a comprehensive programme of school reform, individual changes must be staged

No single change is as effective as a combination of several. A planned programme of school improvement for "at risk" children is best seen as a series of reforms. The word "series" is used deliberately: introducing several reforms simultaneously is too disconcerting. Moreover a stepwise programme has the advantage of retaining interest and enthusiasm.

Short-term improvement is an illusion: good programmes take time to plan, implement and monitor

Reform takes time. Politicians wanting quick results from changes to schools will be disappointed: the time-scale of the programmes in these case studies is usually one of years. It would not be unrealistic to think of a time-horizon of a decade or more before the novel becomes the norm and schools for children who are the concern of this report demonstrate clear evidence of the effects of reform.

References

OECD (1991), *Education and Cultural and Linguistic Pluralism*, CERI/CD(91)15, free document, Paris.

STERN, D., RABY, M. and DAYTON, C. (1992), *Career Academies: Partnerships for Reconstructing American High Schools*, Jossey Bass, San Francisco.

The following documents have not been published, but are available at the OECD or in the concerned countries:

1. *America 2000: The President's Education Strategy,* 1991.
    Press Secretary, White House, Washington, DC.

2. United Kingdom: *National Report*, England, 1991.

3. United States: *Practices for Children and Youth "at risk" of School Failure,*
    McCollum, H., prepared by Policy Study Associates for US Department of Education, 1991.
    Titles of different chapters:
    a)   "Reading Recovery".
    b)   "Success for All".
    c)   "The Academy Model".
    d)   "The Accelerated Schools Model".
    e)   "The School Development Programme, or Comer Process".
    f)   "School Based Management Programmes".

4. Canada (Manitoba):
    a)   *Early School Years*, 1991.
    b)   *Reading/Writing Immersion*, 1991.
    c)   *A School Based Approach to Parent Involvement with Children*, 1991.

5. Portugal: Case study for OCDE/CERI report, Director-General of Basic and Secondary Education, 1991.
    a)   "School in the Inter-cultural Dimension".
    b)   "Interministerial Programme for Promotion of Success in Education (PIPSE)".

6. France:
    a)   *Structures d'accueil des jeunes enfants en milieu interculturel*, Combes, J., 1992.
    b)   *The Priority Education Area ("ZEP") Policy. A Response to the "children at risk" problem*, Best, F., 1992.

7. Netherlands: *How to Motivate Children to Read*, Haan, M. and Kok, W.A.M., Institute for Educational Research.

8. United States: *The Comprehensive Competencies Programme*, C.S. Mott Foundation, Virginia.

    a)   *Competency Based Education: Reshaping American Education*, 1991.

    b)   *Use of the Comprehensive Competencies Programme*, US Basics, 1991.

9.   Portugal: *Children and Adolescents "at risk"*, National Report.

10. United States: *The Teen Outreach Programme*, C.S. Mott Foundation, Virginia.

    a)   *The Teen Outreach Programme*, New York, 1991.

    b)   *Teen Outreach: The Fifth Year of National Replication*, 1991.

    c)   *Process Evaluation of Teen Outreach Programme*, Allen, J.P. and Philliber, S., 1991.

11. Belgium: *Case study*, Duyer, W., Pedagogischer Bureau, National Secretariaat van het Katholiek Onderwijs, Brussels, 1991.

12. Netherlands and Scotland: *The Partnership in Education Project*, Strathclyde, Scotland, Van Leer Foundation, Netherlands, and Strathclyde Regional Council, Scotland, 1990.

13. Germany: Reports from the Freudenberg Foundation.

    a)   *To Live Together and Learn from Each Other: Turkish Children and Mothers Enter School*, Trepte, C., 1991.

    b)   *Weinheim Pupils' Support Group*, Schmidt, GB, 1991.

14. Belgium: *Les enfants et les jeunes "à risque"*, Van Calster, L.L.M., 1991.

15. Australia:

    a)   *Children and Youth "at risk": Effective Programs and Practices*, Australian Conference of Directors-General of Education and The Commonwealth Youth Bureau, Department of Education, Employment and Training, 1991.

    b)   *The Interagency Referral Process, A Core Study*, 1991.

16. Germany: *School Social Work and the Welfare State*, Rademacker, H., 1992.

17. Netherlands: *Reducing Educational Disadvantages: Developments in the Educational Priority Programme in the Netherlands*, Kloprogge, J., Institute for Educational Research, 1991.

18. United Kingdom: *Teaching Children "at Risk" of Educational Failure: The Challenge for Secondary Schools*, 1991.

19. Italy:

    a)   *Research on Drop-outs in the Framework of Palermo*, Mangano, F., 1991.

    b)   *Subjects at Risk of "Dropping out": Definition, Detection, Problems*, Gentile, M.C., 1991.

    c)   *Research Action within the School System: Teachers, Involvement, Training, Action*, Mazzola, C., Mignosi, E., Savagnone, M., Siino, P. and Valenti, D., 1991.

    d)   *The Research-Action: the Family*, Amico, M.C., d'Angelo, V., Diana, M.A. and di Salve, S., 1991.

    e)   *Research-Action within the School System: Students Involvement, Training, Action*, Bomura, R.M., 1991.

    f)   *Examinations and Certifications in Italy: A Balance between Past, Present and Future*, Bucalossi, M.M., 1991.

    g)   *Social Health District*, Cardella, A., Miragliotta, F., Monsurro, R., and Sanfratello, E., 1991.

    h)   *Interventions for the Prevention of Risk Situations: The Integration of Services in the Albergheria Quarter*, Natoli, D., Palermo, 1991.

    i)   *Intervention to Prevent Situations at Risk: The Integration of Services in the Albergheria Quarter*, Puglisi, G., Palermo, 1991.

    j)   *Interventions for the Prevention of Risk Situations: The Integration of Services in the Albergheria Quarter*, Scordato, D.C., Palermo, 1991.

k) *Action for the Prevention of Risk: Co-operation between Social Services – Zen District*, Bruno, A., 1991.
l) *Understanding the Social, Economic and Environmental Context: Instruments Used and Data Gathered*, La Rosa, S. and Villa, E., 1991.

Chapter IV

Transition from School to Work

by

Hermann Rademacker
Deutsches Jugend Institut, Munchen
and
Peter Evans
CERI, OECD, Paris

Introduction

The case studies reviewed in this chapter are concerned with facilitating the transition to work of children and youth "at risk" (CYAR).

In western industrialised societies the vast majority of people can only realise their economic potential through paid work. Therefore success or failure in the transition from school to work is, for most people, central to their economic and social success.

The first placement when entering the labour market can determine the ultimate vocational path as well as the social status which a person can attain. After having made this choice, second and third chances are rarely offered. This is especially true for those who start with low levels of vocational qualifications. Some of the case studies refer to the biographic importance of transition when they claim that access to employment, training, and educational opportunities remains the key determinant of the quality of life available to young people (Australia).

Especially in the most advanced economies the last few decades have been characterised by changes in the labour market which have resulted in an increased risk for unqualified or low qualified members of the labour force. One of the Canadian case studies (Ontario) refers very explicitly to this development. It notes that:

- changes in the market place associated with increased use of modern technologies and work practices;
- a tendency towards the cutting of companies' work forces in contrast to the creation of job entry opportunities; and
- demographic shifts based upon gender, all combine to make the transition process an exceptionally difficult period for adolescents.

Increased qualification standards for employment in modern industry and in the services sector, combined with a rapid decrease in the amount of low qualified labour, result in growing employment risks for all of those who do not meet these new standards.

This is a phenomenon which is readily visible in the most advanced economies, and is now emerging in less technically advanced countries where the expanding industry and services sectors and the modernisation of traditional agricultural production means rationalising large numbers of traditional jobs.

What all of these developments have in common is that they challenge the education systems of those countries which are affected. The general assumption in all the case studies included here is that most schools have not yet realised the full implications of this challenge or at least have not yet found the proper answer to it. Transition from school to work, therefore, still has to become, as the Ontario case study suggests, an issue upon which attention is increasingly focused. This means not only that school has to prepare students better for the transition from school to work, but also that it has to take on a responsibility for students who leave or have already left school. A position also recognised by the French authorities.

The transition from school to work for CYAR may be the last chance for creating the necessary prerequisites for independent membership of society. Thus all support for CYAR, from early childhood to leaving general education, must have, as one of its main goals, successful transition to work, as well as taking account of a wide variety of possible adult roles. Young people who fail to make a successful transition often turn to criminal activities, frequently involving drugs, and have increased risk of health problems including sexually transmitted diseases and AIDS.

Description of the programmes, services or projects included

Youth Access Centre (Australia)

The development in Australia of Youth Access Centres (YACs) constitutes a country-wide, locally based programme supporting transition by means of information, advice and referral. These centres help to improve the local support structure by co-ordinating the activities of related services, especially those of schools, vocational education and training, labour administration, and youth services. They are characterised by:

- an integrated approach both within school, vocational education and training as well as in the wider community;
- the use of strategies to empower students and young people and to encourage parental involvement; and
- a flexible organisational structure.

With other Australian programmes for young people "at risk" they offer two other facilities:

- Improved access to information and advice by the establishment of locally based services which provide comprehensive, co-ordinated information on employment, occupations, education, income support and community services.
- Access to adequate income support which in recent years has been changed quite significantly by the Australian federal government with regard to both the structure and the rates of payments to young people – these changes to an income support structure complement the government's objectives of encouraging young people to undertake post-compulsory education and training.

More than 110 YACs are located in metropolitan and provincial centres across Australia, most of them located in Commonwealth Employment Services (CES) offices alongside other outlets such as Job Placement Centres and Special Service Centres. Most of them operate with three members of staff.

While the Australian programme started with an experimental phase, the Youth Access Centres were from the beginning established within the context of a national policy. They started with experimental establishments which were intended to become model institutions for a regular country-wide structure. Thirty-seven of the 110 Youth Access Centres (in excess of 110 exist as of now) were established in 1985 on a trial basis in Job Centres. They were in areas of identified high youth need. Following a favourable evaluation in 1988/87 a further 16 were opened, and in 1990 another 20 (as part of the Government's Youth Social Justice Strategy). Additional ones resulted from the Client Services Reform of the CES which made use of the experience collected from the successful Youth Access Centres network.

The Youth Entry Programme (Winnipeg, Canada)

The Youth Entry Programme is a special programme in the Winnipeg Core Area Initiative. It is addressed at an historically new group of very "high risk" South-east Asian refugee youths who exhibited various symptoms of emotional and psychological distress due to flight and resettlement. They were largely deprived of material, psychological and family support as they arrived in Winnipeg either as unaccompanied minors, or with broken families. For 15 of them, a 52-week course combining academic training, job experience and counselling was organised. The programme is intended to become a model project for similar support activities for the target population. It takes an interdisciplinary perspective by integrating and making use of the knowledge bases and support potentials of education, mental health, employment and immigration services to meet the complex therapeutic, academic, and financial needs of its clients. An evaluation of this programme then made it possible to identify changes and improvements for further courses.

Student retention and transition in Ontario high schools (Ontario, Canada)

This is a research project, carried out in six school boards in Ontario, which is funded under contract by the Ministry of Education. It focuses on the social ecology of high schools as well as on their organisational characteristics. Six school boards in the province of Ontario participated in the study. All staff in all the secondary schools in these six school boards received questionnaires. Thus data were collected on 95 schools although for most statistical analyses data from only 58 regular high schools were used. Data from approximately 2 250 questionnaires were aggregated on the school level for analytic purposes. In addition, seven school sites in four school boards were selected for case studies. In one northern school board a single school was chosen; in the other three boards, schools with unexpectedly high and unexpectedly low dropout rates were paired. Also different characteristics of the schools were taken into account for these case studies. Thus, in one school board, two schools serving a broad range of students, were selected. Two other vocational schools serving primarily those students who do not aim at post-secondary education were also selected.

High school academies (United States of America)

High School Academies (see also Chapter III) are organised as a school-within-a-school for disadvantaged youth. Nowadays they aim selectively at under-achievers who find improved learning conditions through a curriculum with an emphasis on vocational orientation. Co-operation with business is an important characteristic which provides the opportunity of job experience.

These Academies represent alternatives to the standard organisation of schooling in American secondary education. They offer fundamental academic training combined with training in basic work skills as well as orientation and training for specific occupational areas. They aim at the encouragement of disadvantaged youth to complete high school and to prepare for entering the work place, although the option of attending post-secondary education remains open. Other main characteristics are:
- support from local business and public sector employers, who help with curriculum development, guest speakers, mentors, and work experience positions;
- a selection of students who, firstly, have the potential to succeed in school but whose past performance suggests that they may drop out and, secondly, who express a commitment to training in the occupational area offered by the academy;
- clearly defined rules accepted by students, teachers, parents and administrators;
- paid work experience for qualified students; and
- school and district support for the programme.

Since the first High School Academy was opened in Philadelphia in 1969, other Academies have been developed in a number of sites around the United States. The largest network exists in California where 49 Academies have been established. They prepare their students for a broad range of careers including electronics, auto mechanics, health, the media and computer technology. One of the newest, located in Pasadena, offers training in space technology. During this expansive development they have also changed their target group which in the original Academy consisted of the most disadvantaged and deprived youth in the area served by the school.

The Academies are members of a network. They share common educational, organisational and political ideals. The Academies might be described as part of a movement which expanded through the voluntary adoption by school boards and single high schools of a convincing model. The model was modified according to the specific challenges and conditions in the area served by each new Academy, such as the framework conditions set by the hosting high school, and local opportunities for co-operation with business.

In Philadelphia from 1970-1988 each Academy programme was managed by its own Board of Directors and by the Board of Directors of the Philadelphia High School Academy Association. In 1988 these were merged into one single organisation, the Philadelphia High School Academies, Inc. (PHSA). The 32-member PHSA Board of Directors brings together representatives from the school district, labour, business and the community, to set policy for the Academies.

Each Academy programme is managed by its own Board of Governors made up of upper-level and mid-level business managers, labour leaders, university staff and community leaders. The responsibilities of these boards include the development of day-to-day operations, budgets and links with the private sector.

The PHSA President and a 12-person staff are located in the Association's offices in downtown Philadelphia. In addition to assistance for the Academies, especially during their initial phase of development, three staff members have full-time responsibility for co-ordinating employment opportunities for students.

The Financial Services Academy in Portland, Oregon, is governed by an Advisory Board whose members represent the business community and youth services agencies. The principal role of the board is to review Academy operations and to assist in arranging summer job placements and recruiting adult mentors.

The common element in all the Academies is their relative autonomy, and intensive and institutionalised co-operation with business. Even though the Academies movement is expanding there is at present, no plan to make it a country-wide network.

The Mannheim Project (Germany)

The Mannheim Project was developed in 1983 when the gap between young people demanding apprenticeships and places being offered had reached a maximum. It was part of an initiative started and supported by one of the member states of the then Federal Republic of Germany, Baden-Wurttemberg. It made use of funds coming from the Transition Programme of the European Community, the Federal Government, the City of Mannheim and the Freudenberg Foundation. Since 1987, after the experimental project had finished, the Mannheim Project was continued by the *Land* Baden-Wurttemberg, the city, and the Foundation. With its continuation, new tasks have been taken on and old ones have been expanded. This was made possible because of a new programme, "Youth-Labour-Future", launched by Baden-Wurttemberg for unemployed young people and those at high risk of unemployment. As the project concentrates especially on immigrant youth, it was supported also by the commissioner for foreign inhabitants who is active in Mannheim and in many other German cities.

This is a social work project run from a shop in the centre of the City of Mannheim which acts as a base for its "street work" activities. The project offers counselling on a broad range of problems, and refers young people to special services, schools and providers of vocational education and training. The project functions as a link between foreign young people and their families on one hand and German agencies like schools, administrative services and companies on the other. Since the project participates in the programme "Jugend-Arbeit-Zukunft" (Youth Labour-Future), launched by the *Land* Baden-Wurttemberg, co-ordination on the local level is mandatory, and organised by the youth welfare administration of the city. Because of this the exchange of information and the co-operation with other providers has been improved. As is typical for the "street work" method of social work the young people are counselled at their meeting places in the city.

It is important to note a special component of the work in Mannheim which concentrates on "street work" with Turkish youths. It was established as one component of integrated regional measures for reducing youth unemployment in the city. For the reintegration of the target group, whose members mostly have already experienced several stages of social segregation, their re-entry into paid labour is of central strategic importance. To realise this, the whole repertoire of social and personal support for these people has to be activated.

Drifters – work with youth "at risk" (Niederursel, Germany)

In a "hof", with different craft workshops and other opportunities for work and learning, twelve places for young people aged from 17 to 24 are offered residential training for a ten month period in an anthroposophic* community.

The term "drifters" refers to young people whose problems are not really pathological in nature or socially aberrant but who have failed up to now to find their way into the world of work.

The young people selected suffer from severe psycho-social problems ranging from a history of drug and alcohol abuse to anorexia and attempted suicide. They are described as having in common a fundamental disorientation and "homelessness". They often come from broken homes but not necessarily from poor or disadvantaged families.

The aims of the orientation year at Niederursel go far beyond vocational orientation and learning using work experience mainly as a means for personal development. According to the anthroposophic philosophy, the work experience offered is concentrated on kinds of work which allow for a high degree of personal identification with the activity and its results. Therefore, craftwork and tasks with aesthetic quality dominate.

---

* An educational approach developed by Rudolf Steiner, and based on Christian ethics. It is intended to educate the whole person bringing together cognition, feeling and will, and by giving the person a balanced sense of his position with respect to society and work.

The facility is run by a staff with different qualifications. One is qualified in both joinery and therapeutic pedagogy; the others provide career-related training courses and artistic seminars.

Young people have to apply for a place in the "hof", and this is not made easy for the applicant. Besides a detailed handwritten curriculum vitae, a lengthy orientation talk and a trial week, the applicant has to pay DM 1 700 (around United States $ 1 000) for the ten month period. This self-motivated decision is seen as "the corner-stone of the orientation process".

After leaving the "hof", some follow the courses of education from which they had previously dropped out, and others begin vocational education and training related to the experience and orientation that they acquired at the "hof". The facility tries to keep contact with those who have left, and also tries to give limited additional support to them – if needed, if accepted, and if within the means available. However, if young people regress to their earlier situation there is no further commitment on the part of the "hof".

Federal Youth Aid Programme (Germany)

The Federal Youth Aid Programme in Germany is one of the few instruments through which the Federal Government influences youth services and gives financial support to them. Support for young people in the transition from school to work has gained importance within this programme, especially since the early 1970s when a shortage of apprenticeships associated with a crisis on the labour market started to affect the dual system of vocational education and training. Several experimental programmes, each running for several years, were launched in this field. Each one focuses on specific aspects of support services for integration into the labour force, such as different target groups (*e.g.* women, young foreigners).

The present phase of the experimental programme runs from 1989 until 1993, which is the subject of the case study and includes projects which:

- Aim at and participate in structures for improved co-operation and co-ordination with other services for the orientation, qualification and employment of young people at the local level.
- Try to develop strategies, intended to prevent the segregation of disadvantaged young people into youth service measures. In spite of expanding opportunities on the labour market which existed at the time the report was written, many young people remained caught in these services without finding their way into regular training and employment.

The participating projects have to apply for a subsidy which covers only part of their costs. During the present phase of the programme 54 projects are involved.

The political aim of these experimental programmes is to give incentives and information to the legally responsible executive youth service agencies operating at the local level. The programmes therefore normally include a research element which, in a co-operative way, aims at the evaluation of the projects.

Inter-ministerial Programme for Promotion of Success in Education (Portugal)

The Inter-ministerial Programme for Promotion of Success in Education (PIPSE) in Portugal, in contrast to the high school academies, is a country-wide political action programme for educational reform which in turn forms part of an even larger endeavour of economic and social development in that country. It was established under conditions which did not allow for time-consuming experimentation. PIPSE is co-ordinated by an Inter-ministerial Council acting at the national level and District Management Committees representing the relevant governmental authorities at the regional level. The basis of the educational reform is the Basic Law of the Educational System, passed in October 1986, which has been followed by various decrees since 1987.

The "vocational and prevocational initiative" is one of ten elements in an emergency plan which within a four year period aimed to give support to children who at the age of 13-14 still attended first cycle school (grade 1-4 of primary education). The intention was to overcome failure either by reintegrating these children into the ordinary education system or by enabling them to enrol in a prevocational training course in the hope that they might find an incentive to learn. After starting the programme, employment counselling and vocational guidance were integrated. As a result the programme could orientate itself to pupils' preferences and attitudes as well as local labour market conditions.

The reform addresses school facilities and functioning, educational content and methods, training and further training of teachers, quality and accessibility of school textbooks, curricula and also teacher-student interaction.

The problems to be addressed range from nutrition and insufficient health services for children, to child labour and the limited contacts between schools, families and communities. The prevocational courses accept 13/14-year-old students who have not even completed a minimum of the first cycle curriculum.

The "vocational and prevocational initiative" within PIPSE was part of a wide-ranging reform of a neglected educational system. In such a situation, a country-wide action programme seems to be an appropriate political response. Further differentiation and development may follow after the first effects of the programme have become visible.

Types of programme

The programmes described in the case studies vary in a number of ways. If the transition from school to work is viewed as a biographical process one can differentiate programmes according to their biographical location. Programmes may apply to young people

- before they enter the transition phase (preparatory);
- while they are in supporting programmes; or
- after they have passed through it, *i.e.* reintegrative programmes.

Preparatory programmes

These are programmes addressing school age youth that aim to:
- provide qualifications to improve individual chances on the labour market; and
- improve, during post secondary education, vocational orientation by work experience, and/or counselling and guidance, and by training in marketable job skills.

Examples of these programmes are the High School Academies (United States) and also the labour related aspects of PIPSE.

Supportive programmes

These are programmes that operate during an extended phase of transition and address young people who have already left school. They are supportive in the sense that they try to help young people to be successful in the process in which they are engaged or to integrate them into one of the institutions or agencies which structure the transition from school to work (*e.g.* vocational schools or colleges, training schemes, apprenticeships or entry jobs in companies).

These schemes may compensate where jobs or apprenticeships are unavailable. In addition, they may offer vocational training to young people who have not succeeded in finding work or entering post secondary vocational education, or who may have lost their jobs. A number of the projects covered by the Federal Youth Programme for disadvantaged young people (Germany), and the Government's Youth Strategy (Australia), are examples.

Reintegrative programmes

These programmes address unemployed young people who have already failed in their attempt to gain entry into the labour market. These young people are either severely threatened by social segregation, or have experienced it already. In most cases it is necessary to rekindle a desire for learning, to prevent delinquency, to help them to regain self-esteem, and to stabilise their social situation. It is necessary to continue with a number of social support measures for housing, debt, partnership and family problems and problems with various organisations or authorities including, the courts and the police. One common characteristic of this type of programme is that they are not selective with regard to the young people with whom they work. The programme which fits most clearly into this category is the "street work" project to reduce unemployment amongst Turkish youth in the City of Mannheim. They act when they are confronted with or identify youth at high risk. In contrast, some programmes categorised above either deliberately and explicitly (*e.g.* the High School Academies, United States), or unintentionally and more or less in contradiction to their proclaimed objectives (*e.g.* some of the projects in the Federal Youth Aid Programme, Germany), "cream off" clients from the various "at risk" groups. In this way they have participants in their programmes and effective courses which they can offer which are within the means that they have at their disposal.

Even amongst reintegrative programmes, however, there are some which are highly selective. The "drifters" project (Niederursel) is an example where there is a selection process, and the action that each young person has to take within the programme is a fundamental part of the pedagogical and therapeutic process. The concept underlying this project does not fit *all* young people with similar problems.

Socio-political classification

Another important categorisation which can be made is socio-political. This classifies programmes or measures according to their target groups. Programmes can be divided into two types:

> *i)* those which are related to or are part of *country-wide reform* initiatives to improve the chances of all young people to make successfully the transition from school to work, but with a special concern for the needs of "at risk" groups; and
>
> *ii)* *special programmes* for particular "at risk" groups which are probably only temporarily in need of special support.

Country-wide reform

Country-wide reform initiatives recognise the significance of changes in society, the economy and the labour market for the situation of individuals. Their aim is to enable young people to meet the new demands for a successful transition to work under changing background conditions. In such programmes, in principle all young people are seen as needing additional public support. However, CYAR need to be given special priority.

Under this heading comes the Youth Access Centre Network (Australia) which has a focus on the needs of the disadvantaged, but is not limited to them and (PIPSE) in Portugal. However, PIPSE differs from YAC in two main respects. First, educational reform is embedded in an even larger programme of fundamental economic and social development in that country, and second, the transition component clearly addresses disadvantaged youth as a first priority.

Special programmes

The Federal Youth Aid Programme although initiated and financially supported by the federal government, is a series of locally based special projects for identified "at risk" groups. For the phase of the programme which the case study describes, the integration of the projects into regional networks of social services is a specific objective.

The Winnipeg initiative for Asian refugees and the project in Mannheim for Turkish youth are other examples of special programmes which focus on integrating or reintegrating particular groups within the community who have already become, or are in the process of becoming, socially segregated.

The Student Retention and Transition Project in Ontario high schools needs a special categorisation as an investigative activity to identify reasons for different rates of student retention and successful transition to work in different high schools (Ontario).

Needs and problems identified by the case studies

To different degrees the case studies describe solutions to needs and problems, which threaten successful transition from school to work. These problems have to do with changes in society resulting in particular from economic developments which have followed a common course and which have been noted above. However, when analysed in more detail they often become indicators for relevant and important differences between societies whose economic development is similar.

The Ontario case study refers to the fact that unemployment rates among youth aged 15-24 in Canada are, as in many other countries, traditionally higher than that of the general population. During 1981-1985 they ranged from 11.5 per cent to 17.8 per cent approximately 50 per cent higher than the general rate. Despite a favourable situation in Southern Ontario with figures of 9.3 per cent for youth and 5.5 per cent for general unemployment, the employment situation of young people has deteriorated and is likely to remain depressed.

Increasing numbers of students are dropping out of Ontario high schools. Studies in seven schools revealed that their annual drop-out rates had increased from an average of 10.6 per cent in 1984-85 to 15.3 per cent in 1986-87. This is seen as a serious disadvantage for the transition process from school to work where success mainly depends on three prerequisites:

  i) the guidance or channelling of students;
  ii) the individual's selection of an occupation; and
  iii) the employment opportunities available.

Dropping out of school in most cases occurs as a result of marginalisation during secondary education. However, this is not the whole story and, especially in economically prosperous regions, opportunities in the labour market may also contribute to school drop out. These include for example night shift jobs in warehouses, and summertime construction work, which can be as well or better paid than junior teaching jobs in Canadian school boards. However, even in prosperous regions such jobs seldom survive the next economic crisis. In general, recent changes in the economic and employment structure of western societies have made it more difficult for youth to become integrated into the labour market and schools are frequently insensitive to their problems.

The case studies revealed that schools tend to care more for those students who leave secondary education for colleges and universities than for those who aim at a direct transition from school to work. They often keep in touch with the former after they have left school, while the latter often are not tracked at all. Co-operative programmes and

123

work experience programmes assist a minority of students. Part-time work is a major component in many students' lives. In some schools up to 90 per cent of the students work. Working time varies between 17 and 30 hours per week. The weekly disposable income is believed to be United States $ 75-100, money which is often used for clothing, cars or entertainment, although in many cases it is a necessary support for the students. Work affects their commitment to education – often negatively – and normally does not turn out to be a valuable labour experience which can be used for strategic career planning.

Schools often do not realise the dramatically increased risk of career failure that school drop outs have to face as a result of these recent structural changes. The position that "drop outs, like the poor, will always be with us" is no longer – if it ever was – acceptable. The "liberal position" that leaves the decision of whether to take advantage of school to the student, is often associated with a positive view of the results of these decisions: the weeding out of difficult students is seen as protecting the education of those who remain.

The need for better access for young people to information, advice and referral with regard to vocational orientation and job placements in Australia was identified by the Committee of Inquiry into Labour Market Programmes report (Kirby Report, 1985). These kinds of services complement or replace the support and influence families and the communities have traditionally given by setting a framework for the socialisation of children and youth. This support also provides a vocational orientation for the majority of the young generation. Not only have changes in the family, and in its ability to take care of the integration of children into the labour market, generated this need, but also fundamental changes in the labour system itself. The authors of the Ontario case study quote from "The Forgotten Half: Non-College Youth in America" and noting these trends which apply to all modern western economies:

> "Stable, well paid jobs which do not require advanced training are rapidly disappearing. Between 1979 and 1985, the United States suffered a net loss of 1.7 million manufacturing jobs (...). A highly competitive technological economy can offer prosperity to those with advanced skills, while the trend for those with less education is to scramble for unsteady, part-time, low paying jobs (p. 1)."

In addition to this kind of general need the authors of the case study on High School Academies (United States) refer to studies and reports revealing significant deterioration in living conditions during the last decade for the poorest citizens, many of whom are children. They point out, that on one hand many of the conditions experienced by children living in poverty have a direct impact on their schooling, and on the other that schools with large numbers of poor children are often consumed with problems that go well beyond academics. The scenario they outline for the living conditions of poor children and their schooling is based on factors and developments such as:

- high mobility, especially of low income families, which results in high annual turnover rates in the schools where they are concentrated;
- inadequate nutrition and health care with strong negative consequences for classroom learning; and

– many students living in single parent families which have too little income to supplement school materials, and where the language used at home is often not English.

Schools are typically unequipped to compensate for these conditions. The situation is often worsened by the fact that they are placed in areas plagued by violence and the drug trade. Many of these schools are poorly resourced with insufficient materials and poor student teacher ratios. As they often perform badly, as assessed by standardised test scores, many of them are subject to tight district controls which restrict their chances of finding adequate answers for the problems they are presented with.

The authors then pose some critical questions with respect to concepts of school reform. These address the issues of "excellence", through raised standards for both students and teachers, from the point of view of disadvantaged students. In the absence of instructional reform and further assistance, these children are seen as being least likely to benefit.

The Mannheim Project indicates high unemployment rates in a city where 16 per cent of residents are foreign. In a period of increasing unemployment, and decreasing apprenticeship places for young people, the vocational opportunities for foreign youth in traditional industries are particularly in danger.

A different category of "at risk" youth is served by the "drifters" project (Niederursel). Its clientele frequently comes from broken homes and not from either poor or disadvantaged families. The training offered uses work experience as a means for personal development and focuses on aesthetic activities.

Socio-political contexts

The major social and economic changes already mentioned are common to most countries. But the socio-political contexts within which school-to-work transitions occur are different. These contexts set the framework for the availability of funds and resources that can be mobilised for initiatives and measures to support the transition from school to work, they constitute the climate in which the projects and programmes, described in the case studies, must grow. When learning from each other is one of the aims of the exchange of information and experience between nations regarding support for CYAR, the different socio-political contexts are of special importance. They frame the conditions for the design and delivery of programmes and determine for whom they are intended. For example, in Germany the shortage of apprenticeships within the dual system in the early 1970s led to the instigation of a number of experimental programmes (within the federal youth aid programme), established by the Federal Ministry of Youth, to promote youth services. This contrasts to the establishment of the High School Academies in the United States which developed in response to the violence which erupted in Philadelphia in 1968 and which was seen as a threat to social cohesion. In Winnipeg, the Core area initiative was established as an integrated effort to make co-ordinated use of different funds and programmes for regional development. For the youth entry programme, for south-east Asian refugee youth, this initiative set the framework for the use of funds from the Canada employment and immigration commission, the Winnipeg school division, the neighbourhood services programme, the educational support programme and the employment and training programme of the Core area initiative.

These examples point to the many initiatives that have been stimulated by particular occurrences or problems which need to be interpreted within the different socio-political contexts of OECD Member countries. The extent to which these initiatives are generalisable from one country to another is a matter for debate following careful analysis of common and unique features. The ideas and methods themselves remain relevant, but for success it is likely that they will need reinterpretation into the context of another country.

Target groups

The case studies all display a concern for those who are socially disadvantaged. However, the identified groups differ markedly, with differences relating to the specific characteristics of national societies. Thus besides groups commonly mentioned such as the educationally disadvantaged, the long-term unemployed, the poor, those coming from different cultural or linguistic backgrounds, the homeless, those having suffered from abuse or neglect, and those with low social status, we find special minority groups in specific national or social frameworks such as the Aborigines and Torres Strait Islanders in Australia, South-east Asian refugee youth in Winnipeg, and immigrant Turkish youth in Germany.

The seriousness of the conditions that affect employment opportunities for minority groups can be exemplified with work from Germany on behalf of the Turkish community. Many of these young people, most of them boys, were born in Turkey. Before they came to Germany they often lived in difficult social conditions. Frequently their fathers went to Germany first, and often their mothers followed some years later, leaving the children in Turkey with relatives. Before they joined their parents permanently, some alternated between Germany and Turkey and attended various schools. Their parents often do not live together anymore. Some are divorced and live with new partners often in conditions of great hardship. Young people sometimes do not know where to sleep, and housing problems are common among them.

Many of the males have police files because of shop lifting, car theft or drug dealing, although typically in small quantities. Their meeting places are amusement halls. The "official language", also for the few Yugoslavs, Poles and Italians who belong to the groups, is Turkish. They have much more leisure time than pocket money to spend. They consume little alcohol but frequently hashish. Their interests are driving good cars, wearing expensive clothes and acting "cool".

Many of them get bored when they are told that completing vocational training is the only way of getting a safe job: "That's what everyone has told us, moruk (old man). Do you have anything new to offer?"

After one and a half years of street work two different groups of youths which required two different types of support could be clearly identified:

126

i) The totally neglected with nowhere to live, no money and no access to any kind of support either from relatives or from friends. The project has worked with two young people falling into this category. They needed assistance day and night with all kinds of problems regarding housing and material support, as well as psycho-social help. In the beginning the most serious problem in working with them was to win their confidence; but having won it social workers realised that limits on their actions presented serious constraints. A kind of unconditional involvement was reached which, in these two cases, succeeded in helping them make their first steps towards reintegration into "normal" life-styles. This meant preventing them from becoming imprisoned or from being deported to Turkey.

ii) The semi-neglected do not see themselves as suffering severely. They work occasionally and mostly can stay with their parents. They have small everyday problems and are not aware that they are endangered. The social support for these boys starts with helping them to fill in forms, to write letters and applications, and to meet important deadlines. The relationships established in this way are then used to motivate them to obtain vocational qualifications and to prevent them from getting into trouble. For those who had been in trouble with the juvenile courts, and whose sentences had been suspended, the social worker had taken on the job of probation officer.

However, what both groups have in common, is that their relations with their parents are disturbed in a very specific way. Turkish parents do not see any reason for maintaining any kind of relations with their sons (daughters are not normally affected) after they have withdrawn from their families and their fathers' control. For them, not least because of pressure from other relatives, it is almost impossible to practice an intermediate stage of relations between total integration and subordination, and total separation. This attitude makes them helpless when their children exhibit deviant behaviour and drift beyond their influence, and produces great difficulties in co-operation with social workers.

For the youths it means that they become detached from their social background. The "scene" they join offers ways of solving some acute problems mostly by dealing in drugs. Apart from dealing with these problems, ranging from impending sanctions for truancy or criminal offences to the expiration of residence permits, there is hardly any activity, and they become fatalistic. This fatalism immunises them against pressures to acquire vocational qualifications because that only makes sense within a long term strategy which they say fails to speak to their condition. Social workers wanting to overcome this fatalism need patience, tolerance, and an accurate perception of the right moment to break the fatalistic trap in which the boys are caught.

Early signs of difficult family ties are evident. Sixth and seventh graders become conspicuous by truanting. They visit amusement halls and show up at well known venues for others with similar difficulties. Signals such as these should be taken much more seriously, especially by the inner city schools, and should stimulate action of some kind by school social workers. This should include intensive counselling for the Turkish parents. Preferably the social workers involved should come from the same cultural background. There should be close co-operation between teachers and social workers who need to establish which other services should become involved in order to solve specific problems. This approach can be compared to recent developments in the high school academies.

The first High School Academy in Philadelphia was created to serve the most "at risk" students including a number of legal offenders. Since then the Academies have emerged with a more general programme model to serve students whose school experience and performance indicate that they are not living up to their potential. The data reported for the Academies show that ethnic minorities and those coming from families that are eligible for social welfare programmes are over-represented; in most cases they constitute the majority of the student population. However, the Academies "don't work with kids at the very bottom". Their students "must have the skills, desire, and motivation to go beyond graduation". They do not accept students who have attendance or discipline problems nor those with low grade point averages. Also if parents fail to show a certain level of commitment in assisting their youngsters to succeed in school, those students are not selected. In the Financial Services Academy, special education students are not eligible. According to one teacher, "I would recommend kids who have potential, who can do the work in general math for example (...). Basically, we look for kids who could benefit from structure and support, the kids who have a chance".

The Academies find their students either in the freshman classes of the hosting high school, which means that they come from the catchment area of their hosting school, or, in the case where the host is a magnet school – in up to 20 middle schools inside and outside the catchment area. The Academies recruit according to the rules of the hosting school.

That programmes themselves can distract from a full analysis of the nature of the problem through a process of stigmatisation is brought to the attention by the case study on the Federal Youth Aid Programme in the Federal Republic of Germany. It refers to the problem of stigmatising young people by ascribing them as the targets of social services. The target group in the official description of this programme is defined operationally as those young people and young adults who do not find, or who have severe difficulties finding vocational training and jobs. If references to individual deficiencies are made then these are often described as cognitive, motivational or behavioural deficits. Through a mechanism such as this, disadvantages connected with social characteristics such as sex, ethnicity or nationality, and social status of the family, become individualised and show up as within person deficiencies regarding motivation, qualifications or behaviour. Thus problems of social justice and equal opportunity are transformed into individual problems which then are disconnected from the social structures which contribute to them.

Outcomes and consequences

The outcomes revealed by the different programmes and projects are primarily relevant for the programmes or projects themselves, which constitute the framing conditions for which their results are obviously valid. But projects also offer lessons which can be generalised in varying degrees to other situations. Here we find a spectrum of measures along which the programmes could easily be ordered. At one extreme there are self-contained, wholistic projects, at the other universal, generalisable ones. Both kinds of projects produce experiences others can make use of. But the way of reporting them should and must be different. Up to now the systematic and generalising projects are the ones which have been easier to report on, in papers which may be read at any place at any time. The studies on the more wholistic and self contained programmes usually need to be experienced, by meeting the people acting in them, including participants, clients, and professionals, in order to learn why and how they get the different kinds of acceptance and support they need to survive.

Reaching the target population and effects for the participants

One important aspect of the results is the degree to which the projects reach their target population and meet their different conceptual aspirations. There are examples like the "drifters" project which did not aim to serve its target population exhaustively but presented a specific offer to those who fitted its approach, and were willing to engage themselves in it.

Other projects like the Youth Entry Programme (Winnipeg) are aimed at everyone in the target population but because of limited resources cannot provide for all in one step. They consider themselves successful when they have found enough clients to make full use of the capacities they have at their disposal.

The situation is rather different for programmes like the Mannheim project which act in a certain area where they try to serve all young people "at risk". For this kind of street work project access to the target group is essential. The Mannheim project identified two resources as very effective in supporting and facilitating access to their clients, neglected minority youth:

- A place that can be accessed without fear. In this case it was a computer centre run by a Catholic youth organisation next to the counselling shop of the street workers. This could be accessed easily, and there was a place where no awkward questions were asked, and where the young people could raise their problems, and find competent help.
- A social worker, coming from the same ethnic background as the youth, who speaks their language, comes from the same culture, and is seen as being on their side, but who is also acquainted with the administrative jungle in Germany and knows the appropriate actions to take.

The High School Academies are, as stated earlier, consciously selective with respect to the disadvantaged youth they serve. The selection procedure is quite effective. In 1990, the overall graduation rate of Academy seniors in Philadelphia was 95 per cent. However, considering the number of freshmen who entered the Academies, the graduation rates are less than half of this, since about half fail to complete the two year period of the Academy because of the high mobility and the low incomes of their families. More than half of the graduates found employment and nearly a quarter went on to some form of collegiate education. In Portland in 1991 almost all seniors (25 out of 26) graduated but

17 of the 43 who had started dropped out before they became seniors. The 25 who graduated were all planning to go on to some form of post-secondary education.

The evaluation of the work of the Youth Access Centres shows that they reach 80 per cent of their disadvantaged target groups. Most clients were seeking information related to employment, education and training. A large number were seeking information on and assistance with income support while, in contrast to what was expected, only a few clients (less than 10 per cent) were seeking assistance with social and personal problems. These enquiries were usually referred to another organisation.

However, there are a number of groups of particularly disadvantaged young people for whom access to YAC services is limited. These include those who are severely disadvantaged because of a combination of factors such as very low educational achievement, poor literacy and numeracy skills, long term unemployment, drug and alcohol problems, homelessness, family problems, and membership of specific ethnic groups such as the Aborigines or Torres Strait Islanders.

Given the speed with which it was set up one would not have expected that the *vocational and prevocational initiation* aspect of the PIPSE programme (Portugal) would succeed in reaching all students qualified for it. At the end of the school year 1990/91 only 2 495 (of 7 766 belonging to the target group in the age of 13-14) were involved in prevocational measures.

The reasons were:
- the incompatibility of prevocational education with first cycle schools (grades 1-4 of primary education);
- the lack of local infrastructure to contribute to the measures;
- the geographical dispersion of pupils resulting in time-consuming transportation during normal school hours and difficulties in setting up specific classes for these students;
- the lack of teachers and assistant teachers with an adequate training for this new task;
- misunderstandings about the programme on the parents' side as well as among teachers and administrators, and last but not least; and
- the resistance of some families who needed the income their children could provide by working.

However, there were unexpected positive experiences. Some of the students within the programme attended second cycle schools (while mostly the programme was offered in first cycle schools which are normally attended by pupils aged 6-10) and therefore met their peers. This increased their self-regard and self-esteem. The teachers in these schools had positive experiences and observed that these disadvantaged and sometimes handicapped students were successful. For the parents this created or revitalised expectations of educational success for their children, which in the great majority of cases led them to decide that their children should continue school beyond the first cycle.

In the Youth Entry Programme (Winnipeg) a surprising experience was that the majority of participants chose not to participate in the work component of the programme but pursued academic training so that consequently – and this is interpreted by the authors of the study as "an unexpected positive outcome" – eleven of the participants re-entered the school system while only four re-entered the work place.

Such an outcome indicates discrepancies between the curriculum content of the programme, programme design and goals, on one side and the aspirations of the partici-pants on the other. Thus the authors conclude that the needs and aspirations of the target group should be assessed so that programme objectives, referral selection process, and curriculum content can be designed to correspond to them.

The "drifters" project (Niederursel) has traced its participants. Among the six individuals reported on, one has fallen back into his old ways (drug and alcohol abuse) after finishing his year, while others found ways of living according to the orientation they had developed during their time at the "hof".

Experiences regarding the quality of the services

The Student Retention and Transition research project (Ontario) was aimed at finding differences between more and less successful high schools regarding drop out rates and transition to work. Characteristics of the more successful schools were an openness towards messages and initiatives arising in the environment, an ability and willingness to assess and evaluate this information and a predilection toward innovation, modest risk-taking, and a more pluralistic set of values. They give students multiple choices and opportunities, and convey a supportive, helping perspective. In contrast rigid restrictions and a lack of choice, for example by streaming pupils would suggest the opposite. Whether students are streamed between schools (*i.e.* into colleges, secondary and vocational schools) or within schools (*i.e.* in comprehensive schools with advanced, general and basic streams), the separation creates groups that generate to a marked degree their own sub-cultures. These may be favourable for increasing the chances for some but not for all. This is especially true for disadvantaged students who often are concentrated in the vocational streams which normally get the least attention.

With respect to the transition from school to work, the authors note that labour-oriented activities as part of their general curriculum content were offered by secondary schools up until the mid 1960s. These included extensive courses in vocational, technical, and business education which provided marketable skills or formed respectable appren-ticeship programmes, and they lament that they were terminated after the community colleges were created. This resulted in a vocational qualification gap particularly for those who did not go to college. Changes in technology and in graduation requirements have led to a further decline in technical programmes; only business and marketing courses have survived.

The rapid expansion of co-operative education programmes, which generally have excellent reputations, was not supported by the authors because they mostly remained restricted to the training of specific job skills. They diagnosed a bias amongst the high schools in favour of the advanced main stream. Exit interviews with students leaving without a diploma are the exception rather than the rule. Links to employers and employment agencies tend to be much weaker than comparable ties to post-secondary institutions. The world of work is seen often as the competition that interferes with a student's education rather than as a set of experimental settings that can be truly educational.

The authors propose to make use of existing facilities within the schools to offer the types of experience that students want, such as running a student business. The construction of cottages as part of community oriented packages, for example, could provide the opportunity to earn and to learn; food services training programmes in vocational schools could result in far better eating for students and staff. Schools should compete with the outside world of business and labour and should try to establish similar kinds of incentives so that students have good reasons to develop the same kind of attitudes towards school as they do towards work and business.

The evaluation of the Youth Access Centres confirmed that they have contact with most other youth service providers on the local level. Schools are the main field of activity for the YACs with priority given to those with low retention rates and high proportions of "at risk" students. Contacts with careers teachers are especially strong. With other youth services there is also an exchange of information, referral of clients, and joint membership of inter-agency committees. However, the YACs co-ordination activity, in such networks, varies greatly and in many cases YACs do not undertake a strong co-ordinating role for the youth services in the local area.

The evaluation found that the success with which YAC services meet the needs of the target group is inextricably linked to their ability to function as part of the local youth service network. Co-ordination activities – where they have taken over this role – have contributed significantly to the integration of services, resulting in improved outcomes for young people. The YACs were highly successful at a time when youth unemployment in Australia was at record levels. The comprehensive evaluation of the centres mounted by the Evaluation and Monitoring Branch of the Department of Employment, Education and Training gave ample evidence that the centres are undoubtedly worthy of replication in other countries.

For the Youth Entry Programme various data sources converge to indicate positive growth in emotional, psychological and academic development, positive changes in emotional and moral behaviour and additional benefits for social integration such as adaptation to Canadian life. Students felt more confident about getting along in Canadian society, improved their ability to access assistance from Canadian institutions, and developed coping skills to enable them to solve their difficulties more effectively.

The Federal Youth Aid Programme (Germany) revealed many difficulties and obstacles preventing the achievement of objectives concerned with the development of co-operative structures at the local level. Three ways of planning co-operation were identified, and were evaluated in some detail:

i) *Systematic analyses of the requirements of co-operation and co-ordination in the region*
    Progress on this type of task suffered from two main obstacles: First, the official statistics did not provide all the necessary data on the target groups, on the range of training and employment schemes, and on the development of the regional labour market. Second, the agency carrying out the analysis for the requirement of co-operation was at the same time a part of the structure to be analysed, with

the concern that the results produced could seriously affect already existing relations.

ii) *Initiating co-operation and communication between the providers of existing training and employment schemes*

Communication and co-operation were initiated at one of two levels: either at the staff level or at the management level of the providers of services. Communication at the staff level often produced ideas regarding staff working conditions, and also helped to identify neglect of certain problem areas and target groups. However, there was often limited follow up of initiatives and proposals which emerged. Communication at the management level of the service providers often resulted in increased competition for public money, which is normally only granted over the short term. So when providers seek to establish long-term plans, they tend to divide the available resources, to divide the target populations, and to specify who takes which measures. In this way they tend to strengthen barriers between different providers and services instead of overcoming them.

iii) *Initiating co-operation and communication between all the relevant administrators concerned with qualification and employment policies in the region*

This most ambitious aim for regional transition structures in general is very much in accordance with proclaimed and favoured policies formulated by the European Union, as well as at the national level. In practice, however, at least for the projects covered by this research, it was virtually impossible to detect or develop any effective activity towards this kind of objective. The main obstacles were:

- That the policies formulated at the top levels of administration and government have had hardly any effect at the regional level which supports the related initiatives and services.
- The shortage of professional staff on the projects and the limited time scales for their planning do not favour this type of continuous long term activity. In addition, these regional planning institutions lack authority over the larger service providers, who press for the full use of their existing capacities for vocational training and employment.
- The limited recognition afforded by the labour administration which considers the co-ordination of regional training and employment policies as its own domain.

The school-within-school concept as realised by the High School Academies, has important pay-offs because teachers come to know their students very well, and they take great interest in their lives both inside and outside school. They feel great satisfaction in these relationships and take personal pride in their students' successes. Also the students appreciate having adults they can talk to and they welcome the extended personal relationships.

Higher attendance rates, fewer discipline problems and structured classes make it possible to cover more material and to get the students ready for exams.

The business relations in this network were regarded as very functional and effective: the goal of the work experience segment was to place 85 per cent of the students. The figure was 87 per cent in 1989-90, but because of the deteriorating employment situation in Philadelphia, it was only 80 per cent in 1990-91. Some businesses withdrew their support for student placements because they were either eliminating the positions the students filled or reassigning them to regular employees who might otherwise have been laid off.

Most students who get job placements complete their assignments and receive good reports from their employers. Some are hired by the firms after graduation. Such graduates, according to the teachers, are powerful role models for students who visit the firms as part of the general career orientation activities.

In Philadelphia the Academies are regarded as successful and an expansion is planned from 2 100 students in 1991 to 5 000 in 1996. Schools interested in hosting an Academy are required to submit proposals indicating how they would develop the Academy and how it would contribute to meeting local needs including those of businesses.

Concluding comment

The programmes discussed above, although varying in philosophy, aims and objectives, organisational structure and methods of work all demonstrate effective approaches to helping CYAR make a successful transition to work. Given the problems that they encounter, this represents a great achievement and hints at what could be done if their methods and approaches were implemented on a larger scale, a goal which should have a high priority in policy formulation. Whether the programmes are generalisable or not is a matter for debate. However, the various innovations that have been described all point to the need for especial concern to be given to youth "at risk" in this phase of their lives. And this is an action which can be adopted, in any country, within an appropriately formulated policy framework.

Keypoints

Work is an essential component of individual economic and social success

The vast majority of citizens in OECD Member countries can only achieve their aspirations through paid work. The transition process is therefore vital and career choice is crucial with second and third chances rarely available. This is especially true for those with low levels of vocational qualifications.

The need for increased skills is a challenge to the education system

Most schools have not yet realised the full implications that changes in the labour market demands are likely to make and the transition to work period is not given adequate attention. Good programmes will consider student needs and interests in selecting relevant experiences.

Transition to work programmes have different aims

Transition to work programmes can either be preparatory to entering work or supportive for those who have left school either in the workplace itself or in entering (*e.g.* vocational schools). Or, they can be reintegrative, addressing the problems of young people who have failed in their attempt to enter the labour market.

Transition to work programmes also address different target groups

Some programmes are concerned with country-wide reform initiatives but with special concern for "at risk" groups. Other programmes are aimed at particular groups who are "at risk" and can be short term.

Schools may not keep follow-up records on all of their students

Schools tend to care more for those students who leave for colleges and universities than for those who go to work. Records are often kept on the former but not so frequently on the latter.

Work is often seen as a threat to education

The world of work is often seen as the competition that interferes with a student's education rather than as a set of experimental settings that can be truly educational.

Access to information on vocational orientation and job placement is essential

Young people need better access to good advice on work matters.

Co-ordination of policy is lacking

Quality of service requires good co-ordination of policy objectives at many levels of the system. The involvement of local communities and teachers at the very outset is likely to prove very beneficial.

References

ALTIERI de (1991), *Evaluation of the Youth Entry Programme*, Final Report, funded by the Winnipeg Core Area Initiative, Winnipeg.

BRAUN, F., LEX, T., SCHAFER, H., and ZINK, G. (1992), *The Improvement of the Transition from School to Work for Disadvantaged Young People,* Analysis of a Federal Youth Aid Programme in the Federal Republic of Germany, Munchen, Germany.

HASLAM, M.B. (1991), "High school academies", in McCollum, H. (ed.), *Best Practices for Children and Youth at Risk of School Failure*, six case studies prepared for the US Department of Education, Washington.

KIRBY (1985), *Report of the Committee of Inquiry Unit Labour- Market Programmes*, Department of Employment, Education and Training, Canberra, Australia.

KRAUCH, S., and WITTICH, J. (1991), *Drifters Work with Youth "at Risk"*, Freudenberg Foundation, Weinheim, Germany.

LAWTON, S.B., LEITHWOOD, K.A., BATCHER, E., DONALDSON, E.L., and STEWART, R. (1988), *Student Retention and Transition in Ontario High Schools. Policies, Practices and Prospects*, Ontario, Canada.

REINDEL, H., and TURAN, S. (1992), "Street social work with Turkish youths as a component of integrated regional measures for reducing youth unemployment in Mannheim", mimeographed case study presented to the activity on Children and Youth "at Risk" by the German authorities.

Government reports:

Australian Conference of Directors of Education and the Commonwealth Youth Bureau, Department of Education, Employment and Training, *Children and Youth "at Risk": Effective Programs and Practices*.

Ministry of Education, Office of the Secretary of State for Educational Reform, Inter-Ministerial Programme for Promotion of Success in Education (PIPSE), case study for the OECD/CERI project, *Children and Youth "at Risk"*, Lisbon, Portugal, 1991.

Chapter V

Conclusions and Policy Implications

by

Peter Evans
CERI, OECD, Paris

The concept of "at risk", the concerns and the relation to failure

Children and youth "at risk" (CYAR) are those who come from disadvantaged backgrounds where poverty is a frequent common factor. They are failing to benefit adequately from a country's education system and to become effectively integrated into society. The outcome of this failure can be truly tragic for individuals, families and society alike.

It is clear from the information that has been provided by participating countries that CYAR present a considerable and growing economic and social problem. High levels of unemployment especially among disadvantaged young people, anti-social behaviour, attraction to drugs and crime are examples of a general alienation, identified in the report.

The cause of the problem is now seen as having a strong social developmental component whereby failure to adjust is created by unsatisfactory transactions in the family environment, in school and across the life cycle. "At risk" is not a uni-dimensional concept. There are multiple causes ranging from less than optimal intra-uterine environments that lead to incomplete development and damage before birth to rank social prejudice. But it has been demonstrated that a cumulation of risk factors increases a person's chances of failure multiplicatively. As already said, one factor *e.g.* being from a single parent family may not be too harmful. Two factors *e.g.* single parent family and poverty, increase the chances of a negative outcome by four times. Four factors predict a tenfold increase in the chances of a negative outcome. This is an area in which more information is needed and where there would seem to be room for intensified policy analysis particularly in regard to resource distribution.

Prevention and remediation

In pursuing this work and the reforms that are implied it is important to bear in mind that the education service already operates a number of strategies to help CYAR. These vary among countries and include methods such as repeating a year as well as various other forms of *remedial* action. It is within the general framework of dissatisfaction with these traditional methods and their limited effectiveness that the innovations reported here have been identified. Thus these innovations indicate a shift away from *remedial* approaches to more *preventive* ones, although it must be remembered that remedial interventions at one stage may be for purposes of prevention at the next.

The problems of CYAR have been examined at three stages in the life cycle; during pre-school, school and transition to work. In the pre-school period the importance of developing a preventive approach was emphasised, in particular the need to develop improved child care services especially for those families "at risk"; an intervention at this stage with the family has a preventive purpose for the child. The significance of this period for the future education of the child was noted and in some countries, such as France, there have been active educational steps taken. However, the report notes that in general in Member countries pre-school facilities are inadequate. A further problem area for resolution is to clarify the purpose of pre-school provision in terms of the balance to be achieved between educational goals and care. Developing a broader view of the goals of education at this stage which include the social development of the child would be one way to make progress.

During the period of schooling there is a necessity for schools to develop ways of responding more effectively to their pupils' educational needs. This extends from pedagogic and curricula reform to school management and organisational issues. Many examples of successful innovations in these areas, that respond to children's social and educational needs, have been reviewed. Schools have been "turned round" as a result of the reforms that have been described in the case studies, creating atmospheres and student attainments that schools in favoured areas would be proud of. So what is good for children "at risk" may be good for all children. Much of the work, as for the pre-school period, has an essentially preventive aspect. This is particularly true of the primary years by making sure that children have acquired the basic educational skills. In the later years the projects often had the goal of giving pupils experience of the work place and its social demands in order to widen their horizons for career choice. There is a need to develop high quality services since "at risk" groups are prone to receiving low quality information and support and in certain cases not to use available services at all.

In the chapter on transition to work programmes intended to pick up the pieces of the lives of young people for whom the system has failed to engender social integration were discussed. The world of work is seen often as the competition that interferes with a student's education rather than as a set of experimental settings that can be truly educational. The complexity of the task is evident, often made worse by cultural mores which bring into conflict the traditional family values of ethnic minorities and those of the host nation, commonly taken on by their children, which can have the effect of removing the family, as a support structure, from the young person.

A number of common and rather general themes, which are of considerable significance, emerge. In particular, the need to individualise approaches in socialising and educating CYAR and the need to link together a range of support structures that go beyond the immediately relevant service, for instance co-operation between education and business are noteworthy. However, the practice on the ground is fragmented. In line with the theoretical analyses a move towards a systemic approach can be clearly identified, with a particular need to reunite schools, families and the communities. This important policy goal itself requires co-ordination between the services that address the needs of CYAR in order to provide a smooth continuity of support, both within the various stages and during transitions between them, from birth through to the successful attainment of work.

A range of policy initiatives relating to pre-school, school and transition to work have been identified in the report which vary in comprehensiveness from relatively fragmented efforts to highly co-ordinated approaches. The latter exist most clearly in countries where CYAR have received a relatively high policy profile at central government level such as Australia, France, the Netherlands and Portugal. Other countries are moving in this direction but in yet others a co-ordinated approach has still to emerge. An important factor underlying these differences is the extent to which countries have chosen to develop preventive approaches which require comprehensive inter-departmental and inter-sectoral collaboration and which of necessity need co-ordination at central government level.

The complexity of the issues involved can be illustrated via further discussion on three particular issues: multi-culturalism, the role of the family and of women.

Major issues

The needs of ethnic minority groups require special consideration

Many of the children described as ''at risk'' come from ethnic minority groups who have become permanent features of the developing cultures of OECD Member countries. These peoples bring their own cultures and practices which often contrast markedly with those of the host countries. Not all ethnic sub-groups, of course, constitute an ''at risk'' factor, but where they do problems can be especially acute for children who are brought up in the host nation and take on its traditions. Conflicts that can develop between the children and the family can be devastating and if not dealt with carefully and sensitively can put children in serious jeopardy. There are a number of educational issues such as the teaching of language and the recognition of the significance of the cultures of ethnic minorities that need further consideration. These have been discussed in detail in the CERI study on *Education and Cultural and Linguistic Pluralism* (OECD, 1991).

For many OECD Member countries there has been a growing need over the past few years to pay increasing attention to ethnic minorities. It is clear that this is a highly complex problem and that countries vary greatly in the level and nature of problems to be addressed and in their policy frameworks. Nevertheless, the position of ethnic minorities still presents an immense challenge to the statutory services, and the way that they work, and there is an urgent need to review policies and practices in this area.

The structures and expectations of families are changing and must be taken into account in social actions and school reform

It is well known that family structures have changed and are continuing to evolve, with an increasing number of single parent families and other more complex arrangements. This creates a number of problems which, as Coleman (1991) has pointed out, can seriously restrict the resources the family can provide. By resources Coleman is referring to the concept of social capital, *i.e.* the resources that reside in the social structure itself in norms, social networks, and the inter-personal relationships that contribute to a child's development.

These difficulties are exacerbated by poverty – a frequent context for single parent families and a feature of "at risk" status. As a consequence societies must learn how to compensate for these deficiencies.

But there are other changes that push in a different direction. Families are smaller and planned and in this context parents can devote more interest to each child's emotional, social and educational needs. Thus there is more concentrated concern that each child should be successful or at least develop a well balanced life-style with work playing an important role. And the stakes are higher both for parents and children. This is true for both men and women. Particular issues relating to women are summarised in the next section.

These concerns will inevitably impact on schools especially following policies of accountability which give "power" to parents. And here there is a danger that developments in education and schools will reflect the pressures of parents of non "at risk" pupils at the expense of those "at risk".

Policies and planning must take account of the new role that women are fulfilling in society

The leaders of single parent families are usually women and the poverty that can exist in such circumstances is therefore largely a feminine issue. Women work, often of necessity and with the expectation that they will be able to continue their working lives as soon as their children can be adequately cared for outside the home – an expectation engendered and supported by equity in education. The care of young children is, then, a pressing issue. The signal importance of the early years has been demonstrated in this report. But a second issue has also emerged which has longer cultural roots. In many countries community/family networks exist to find males employment which do not exist for females, who would traditionally be expected to give their labour to family support and development, helping to ensure cultural continuity. The fact that women, even after achieving relative success at school, tend to end up in low paid and low status work is a considerable cause for concern.

Changing the system

Although the information provided concentrated for the most part on educational matters, perhaps the most interesting developments are those which, in an attempt to develop a systemic approach, place schooling into a wider social context. This approach recognises that education is a social responsibility that goes beyond schooling. It follows that a high quality education for all would indicate a high quality (social) environment for all.

Services co-ordination

The country reports and case studies described here provide many examples of ways to respond to the challenges provided by CYAR. It is clear that the problems are more than can be handled adequately by education systems acting alone: a coherent, systems orientation is needed. The implementation of such an approach requires the development of new arrangements which may cut across existing departmental or ministerial boundaries and budgets. Examples of these have been given. They include Inter-agency collaboration in Australia, ZEPs in France, EPAs in the Netherlands, PIPSE in Portugal, ecosystems in Italy. It is worth noting, that collaboration and co-ordination involve services acknowledging, among other things, the limits of their own roles, while at the same time developing awareness of the importance of exchange in maintaining collaboration.

These systemic development projects are in practice community development and action research studies on a massive scale. Their goals are to help local communities to learn how to develop their own dynamic responses to the problems that they face by creating the conditions and skills that are necessary to meet the needs presented by local problems. And this means bringing together services, schools, families, business in a unified attempt to solve the problems of failure and unemployment by providing opportunities to learn about each other's assumptions, values and needs in developing a unity of purpose and a sense of belonging, and in building up the social capital of the community.

The school level

This systemic or wholistic approach has been considered in the context of the development of schools, for instance where the placing of children at the centre of the system leads to the need for more sensitive pastoral and management approaches, as well as curriculum and pedagogic development which is designed to meet the needs of the pupils. Developing school ethos and teacher skills and attitudes are paramount in this process. Continuity between stages of education is another important consideration.

However no school reform is easy to achieve and accepting the need for time in terms of years is vital. It is worth remembering the 25 year time scale of the Better Beginnings Better Futures project from Ontario, Canada.

Individualising the approach

What so many of these innovative programmes are aimed at is the personalisation of processes or the individualisation of teaching in an effort to create a more relevant, sensitive and client-centred approach. It is worth pointing out that individualisation does not mean providing extended opportunities for individual teaching; rather it implies the need for schools to develop flexibility in their responses to pupils. Achieving an individualised approach requires changes in the ways professionals work and think about their pupils. In education it means changes in classroom organisation and school management to allow for the development of flexible teaching methods. Time for thinking and planning new developments, especially for teachers, is also of great importance.

Training of teachers and other professionals

Teacher training, by common consent, needs to be improved not only to help teachers develop appropriate attitudes, but also to foster their skills in individualising the curriculum and in classroom management. This is of particular importance since many interesting developments begin in the classroom, where change is perhaps relatively easy to achieve. A complex challenge here is the way in which the curriculum needs to be developed to allow for cultural differences, especially in language acquisition. This is of special significance since inadequate control of the host nation's instructional language is a major risk factor. These issues have been discussed fully in the CERI study on linguistic pluralism (OECD, 1991).

Improvements in the training courses for all of the professionals involved is required. Developing material understanding of the ways in which various professional groups work would be essential.

Resources and funding

A systems approach has implications for resources and funding. Developing flexibility in resource use and funding and the appropriate targeting of resources are key issues. This is perhaps best achieved by developing methods which allow for devolution to local sites. In the ZEP programme in France, for instance, local sites can apply for additional support to meet local demands which they have identified. The sites are evaluated and accountability can be achieved in this way. In the disadvantaged schools programme in Australia accountability was achieved through certain programme requirements. Most countries recognise that in order to get the additional resources through to the children for whom they are intended, and achieve the goal of individualisation, decisions must be made at the local level. This has the advantage of empowering parents and other local interests by involving them in decisions about programmes and improving relevance.

Definitions and statistics

The concept of CYAR is far from consistent across countries as reflected in the variable prevalence statistics. If countries are to provide extra resources to help those "at risk" to adapt and learn more effectively, then a means is needed to deploy and target resources efficiently and effectively. More and better statistics will be needed. This presents problems since the concept of CYAR is a relative one and related to perceptions of the quality of life that is acceptable to a community. "At risk" status may change over the course of a child's life simply because the parents move house or gain employment, or vice versa. In addition, a cumulation of risk factors has been shown to be multiplicatively related to risk outcome. In following this logic it could be argued that proportionately greater resources should be allotted to those with multiple risk factors, as is done in the Netherlands. However, it is questionable, on the data available in this report, whether single risk factors merit increased resources since the outcomes for these groups have been shown to be the same as those groups with no risk factors. Further research is needed here both to establish the point and the weightings that should justifiably be given to the associated factors in determining funding allocations.

Evaluation

The approaches which have been described in this report are innovative in nature and are frequently, and rightly, the subject of evaluation which is a necessary process in developing co-ordinated approaches across a country as a whole. OECD Member countries' use of systematic evaluation varies substantially, as became clear during the meeting in Washington (OECD, 1992) on the evaluation of programme effectiveness where preferences for different evaluation strategies emerged. Some like the United States were keen on supporting true experimental designs with random assignment of "subjects". Other countries found such an approach ethically difficult and preferred more illuminative designs.

It is more than just ethics, however, which underlies these differences. There is also a lack of agreement on basic principles of evaluation which extends across the whole of social science and which challenges the assumption that causes of change in behaviour can be thought about in the same way as causes in natural science. This is not the place to amplify those arguments but it is important to recognise that the lack of certainty in the choice of method can lead to the importance of evaluation being under-emphasised. This point applies to much of the work included here which was often not evaluated in any very sophisticated manner. Its credibility then rests on whether the results are commensurate with other work or not, and whether the actors see it as useful. In general, both of these conditions appear to be satisfied. Certainly most of the innovations are based on methods and examples that are well grounded in the theories and practice which characterise the academic literature. This applies more strongly perhaps to the specific curriculum development examples than those which emphasise collaboration and systemic approaches. Evaluation, however, is generally regarded as important as a method of providing feedback to help make systems more responsive to their clients and also for accountability.

Evaluation is an important aspect of system design, implementation and generalisation and its use needs to be carefully planned in the constructive development of new approaches. This is another area in need of elaboration since the methods chosen must be commensurately broad in scope and in place over an adequate time scale to reflect system change validly and reliably.

Policy implications

The challenges presented by CYAR and the specific solutions being offered are significant enough to raise the question of rigorous analysis of specific policy initiatives in this area. There is a risk of policy fragmentation and resource waste. New approaches along the lines described, if they are to flourish, require more clarity and coherence in policy making. Such developments have taken place in some countries under a rubric of social justice for all. It has become clear that a high quality education for all involves more than developing policies for the education system alone. The approach to prevention is highly apposite. It includes also a concern with the wider social environment, with prevention as a central concept.

Developing a systemic, preventive approach involves schools, families and communities as well as the inclusion of partners other than the statutory services such as business and foundations in developing supportive frameworks for children from birth through to their integration into the workplace. A policy of local development within a national framework would appear to be the best way of handling the implementation with central governments dealing with overall policy directions, resourcing, assessment and evaluation and the distribution of resources to meet local needs.

This report has adopted an optimistic tone. It has brought together work which has shown what is being done to improve the way in which our social systems function in supporting CYAR to improve their skills and to integrate them successfully into our societies. Much more remains to be done, but the future could look much brighter for many more of today's young people if the policy issues underlying the reforms identified in this report were made more explicit, given greater prominence, and further developed in the framework of national reform.

There is every reason to believe that in the medium to long term these reforms could be cost-effective. Funds put into pre-school education represent an excellent investment in terms of savings on for example remedial and custodial costs later in school and in the post-school period. If collaboration between services is the way forward then cost effectiveness analyses that take into account inter-sectoral inputs and outputs must feature in the evaluative model. This is certainly an area that would be worthy of further investigation.

Key points have been abstracted for each of the chapters and are listed at the end of each one.

References

COLEMAN, J.S. (1991), *Parental Involvement in Education*, Washington.

OECD (1991), ''Education and cultural and linguistic pluralism'', free document, CERI/CD(91)15, Paris.

OECD (1992), ''Conclusions of the Washington meeting, 6-9 May 1991'', free document, CERI/CYR(92)01, Paris.

References

Framework for Country Reports

A. Who is "at risk"?

- size and nature of "at risk" population;
- family and environmental factors that lead to school failure;
- quantification of outcomes associated with being a member of an "at risk" group; and
- national policies – prevention, amelioration and a discussion of resources in each country.

B. Intervention strategies for different age groups

In early childhood

- identification of roles of cognitive and social issues involved;
- quality and scope of care and the nature of services; and
- parental involvement.

In school age population

- effective strategies; and
- effective schools to cover educational issues of content, drill and practice, accelerated curriculum, pedagogy and also management styles and ethos.

C. Transition to work

- special skills needed (*e.g.* special job skills);
- linkage between schools and business; and
- drop-out prevention strategies.

D. General section on cross-cutting issues

- governance;
- organisation of services and inter-agency collaboration;
- delivery mechanisms;
- issues of accountability (are they working, do they reach the intended population?);
- empowerment (*e.g.* choice of school);
- role of community; and
- parental involvement.

Annex 2

Framework for Case Study

The following represents the outline of a structure for the case study reports.

a) The aims of the programme studied:
   e.g. prevention/amelioration with what specific goals?
   Note 1: "programme" may not be the most appropriate term for certain case studies since some people may interpret this as a term to imply a "top-down" approach. The project would not want to discourage the study of self-determined grassroots developments.
   Note 2: where relevant it would be desirable to provide an account of the origin and derivation of the aims of the programme.

b) The target population:
   e.g. pre-school, school age, transition to work, across phase (*e.g.* primary to secondary).

c) The specific context:
   e.g. home, school, work, or a combination of these or other factors.

d) The operation of the programme and the services, etc., used (including resourcing) to achieve the aims, *e.g.* directly with children/young people, or indirectly with parents, professionals, community.

e) The evolution of the programme:
   e.g. initiation, development, maintenance, modification, etc.; whether the programme became institutionalised and if so, how?

f) The evaluation of the (multiple) outcomes of the programme in relation to evolving aims, context, policy, etc.
   Note 1: the evaluation of the programme should not be limited to prior assumptions if additional, and particularly unexpected, considerations are judged relevant.

MAIN SALES OUTLETS OF OECD PUBLICATIONS
PRINCIPAUX POINTS DE VENTE DES PUBLICATIONS DE L'OCDE

ARGENTINA – ARGENTINE
Carlos Hirsch S.R.L.
Galería Güemes, Florida 165, 4° Piso
1333 Buenos Aires   Tel. (1) 331.1787 y 331.2391
                    Telefax: (1) 331.1787

AUSTRALIA – AUSTRALIE
D.A. Information Services
648 Whitehorse Road, P.O.B 163
Mitcham, Victoria 3132   Tel. (03) 873.4411
                           Telefax: (03) 873.5679

AUSTRIA – AUTRICHE
Gerold & Co.
Graben 31
Wien I   Tel. (0222) 533.50.14
                    Telefax: (0222) 512.47.31.29

BELGIUM – BELGIQUE
Jean De Lannoy
Avenue du Roi 202
B-1060 Bruxelles   Tel. (02) 538.51.69/538.08.41
                        Telefax: (02) 538.08.41

CANADA
Renouf Publishing Company Ltd.
1294 Algoma Road
Ottawa, ON K1B 3W8   Tel. (613) 741.4333
                         Telefax: (613) 741.5439
Stores:
61 Sparks Street
Ottawa, ON K1P 5R1   Tel. (613) 238.8985
211 Yonge Street
Toronto, ON M5B 1M4   Tel. (416) 363.3171
                         Telefax: (416)363.59.63
Les Éditions La Liberté Inc.
3020 Chemin Sainte-Foy
Sainte-Foy, PQ G1X 3V6   Tel. (418) 658.3763
                         Telefax: (418) 658.3763

Federal Publications Inc.
165 University Avenue, Suite 701
Toronto, ON M5H 3B8   Tel. (416) 860.1611
                         Telefax: (416) 860.1608
Les Publications Fédérales
1185 Université
Montréal, QC H3B 3A7   Tel. (514) 954.1633
                         Telefax: (514) 954.1635

CHINA – CHINE
China National Publications Import
Export Corporation (CNPIEC)
16 Gongti E. Road, Chaoyang District
P.O. Box 88 or 50
Beijing 100704 PR   Tel. (01) 506.6688
                         Telefax: (01) 506.3101

CHINESE TAIPEI – TAIPEI CHINOIS
Good Faith Worldwide Int'l. Co. Ltd.
9th Floor, No. 118, Sec. 2
Chung Hsiao E. Road
Taipei   Tel. (02) 391.7396/391.7397
                         Telefax: (02) 394.9176

**CZECH REPUBLIC – RÉPUBLIQUE
TCHÈQUE**
Artia Pegas Press Ltd.
Narodni Trida 25
POB 825
111 21 Praha 1   Tel. 26.65.68
                          Telefax: 26.20.81

DENMARK – DANEMARK
Munksgaard Book and Subscription Service
35, Nørre Søgade, P.O. Box 2148
DK-1016 København K   Tel. (33) 12.85.70
                         Telefax: (33) 12.93.87

EGYPT – ÉGYPTE
Middle East Observer
41 Sherif Street
Cairo   Tel. 392.6919
                         Telefax: 360-6804

FINLAND – FINLANDE
Akateeminen Kirjakauppa
Keskuskatu 1, P.O. Box 128
00100 Helsinki
Subscription Services/Agence d'abonnements :
P.O. Box 23
00371 Helsinki   Tel. (358 0) 12141
                         Telefax: (358 0) 121.4450

FRANCE
OECD/OCDE
Mail Orders/Commandes par correspondance:
2, rue André-Pascal
75775 Paris Cedex 16   Tel. (33-1) 45.24.82.00
                         Telefax: (33-1) 49.10.42.76
                          Telex: 640048 OCDE
Orders via Minitel, France only/
Commandes par Minitel, France exclusivement :
36 15 OCDE
OECD Bookshop/Librairie de l'OCDE :
33, rue Octave-Feuillet
75016 Paris   Tel. (33-1) 45.24.81.81
                              (33-1) 45.24.81.67
Documentation Française
29, quai Voltaire
75007 Paris   Tel. 40.15.70.00
Gibert Jeune (Droit-Économie)
6, place Saint-Michel
75006 Paris   Tel. 43.25.91.19
Librairie du Commerce International
10, avenue d'Iéna
75016 Paris   Tel. 40.73.34.60
Librairie Dunod
Université Paris-Dauphine
Place du Maréchal de Lattre de Tassigny
75016 Paris   Tel. (1) 44.05.40.13
Librairie Lavoisier
11, rue Lavoisier
75008 Paris   Tel. 42.65.39.95
Librairie L.G.D.J. - Montchrestien
20, rue Soufflot
75005 Paris   Tel. 46.33.89.85
Librairie des Sciences Politiques
30, rue Saint-Guillaume
75007 Paris   Tel. 45.48.36.02
P.U.F.
49, boulevard Saint-Michel
75005 Paris   Tel. 43.25.83.40
Librairie de l'Université
12a, rue Nazareth
13100 Aix-en-Provence   Tel. (16) 42.26.18.08
Documentation Française
165, rue Garibaldi
69003 Lyon   Tel. (16) 78.63.32.23
Librairie Decitre
29, place Bellecour
69002 Lyon   Tel. (16) 72.40.54.54
Librairie Sauramps
Le Triangle
34967 Montpellier Cedex 2   Tel. (16) 67.58.85.15
                          Tekefax: (16) 67.58.27.36

GERMANY – ALLEMAGNE
OECD Publications and Information Centre
August-Bebel-Allee 6
D-53175 Bonn   Tel. (0228) 959.120
                         Telefax: (0228) 959.12.17

GREECE – GRÈCE
Librairie Kauffmann
Mavrokordatou 9
106 78 Athens   Tel. (01) 32.55.321
                         Telefax: (01) 32.30.320

HONG-KONG
Swindon Book Co. Ltd.
Astoria Bldg. 3F
34 Ashley Road, Tsimshatsui
Kowloon, Hong Kong   Tel. 2376.2062
                         Telefax: 2376.0685

HUNGARY – HONGRIE
Euro Info Service
Margitsziget, Európa Ház
1138 Budapest   Tel. (1) 111.62.16
                         Telefax: (1) 111.60.61

ICELAND – ISLANDE
Mál Mog Menning
Laugavegi 18, Pósthólf 392
121 Reykjavik   Tel. (1) 552.4240
                         Telefax: (1) 562.3523

INDIA – INDE
Oxford Book and Stationery Co.
Scindia House
New Delhi 110001   Tel. (11) 331.5896/5308
                         Telefax: (11) 332.5993
17 Park Street
Calcutta 700016   Tel. 240832

INDONESIA – INDONÉSIE
Pdii-Lipi
P.O. Box 4298
Jakarta 12042   Tel. (21) 573.34.67
                         Telefax: (21) 573.34.67

IRELAND – IRLANDE
Government Supplies Agency
Publications Section
4/5 Harcourt Road
Dublin 2   Tel. 661.31.11
                         Telefax: 475.27.60

ISRAEL
Praedicta
5 Shatner Street
P.O. Box 34030
Jerusalem 91430   Tel. (2) 52.84.90/1/2
                         Telefax: (2) 52.84.93
R.O.Y. International
P.O. Box 13056
Tel Aviv 61130   Tel. (3) 49.61.08
                         Telefax: (3) 544.60.39
Palestinian Authority/Middle East:
INDEX Information Services
P.O.B. 19502
Jerusalem   Tel. (2) 27.12.19
                         Telefax: (2) 27.16.34

ITALY – ITALIE
Libreria Commissionaria Sansoni
Via Duca di Calabria 1/1
50125 Firenze   Tel. (055) 64.54.15
                         Telefax: (055) 64.12.57
Via Bartolini 29
20155 Milano   Tel. (02) 36.50.83
Editrice e Libreria Herder
Piazza Montecitorio 120
00186 Roma   Tel. 679.46.28
                         Telefax: 678.47.51
Libreria Hoepli
Via Hoepli 5
20121 Milano   Tel. (02) 86.54.46
                         Telefax: (02) 805.28.86
Libreria Scientifica
Dott. Lucio de Biasio 'Aeiou'
Via Coronelli, 6
20146 Milano   Tel. (02) 48.95.45.52
                         Telefax: (02) 48.95.45.48

JAPAN – JAPON
OECD Publications and Information Centre
Landic Akasaka Building
2-3-4 Akasaka, Minato-ku
Tokyo 107   Tel. (81.3) 3586.2016
                         Telefax: (81.3) 3584.7929

KOREA – CORÉE
Kyobo Book Centre Co. Ltd.
P.O. Box 1658, Kwang Hwa Moon
Seoul   Tel. 730.78.91
                         Telefax: 735.00.30

MALAYSIA – MALAISIE
University of Malaya Bookshop
University of Malaya
P.O. Box 1127, Jalan Pantai Baru
59700 Kuala Lumpur
Malaysia   Tel. 756.5000/756.5425
                                    Telefax: 756.3246

MEXICO – MEXIQUE
Revistas y Periodicos Internacionales S.A. de C.V.
Florencia 57 - 1004
Mexico, D.F. 06600   Tel. 207.81.00
                                    Telefax: 208.39.79

NETHERLANDS – PAYS-BAS
SDU Uitgeverij Plantijnstraat
Externe Fondsen
Postbus 20014
2500 EA's-Gravenhage   Tel. (070) 37.89.880
Voor bestellingen: Telefax: (070) 34.75.778

**NEW ZEALAND
NOUVELLE-ZÉLANDE**
Legislation Services
P.O. Box 12418
Thorndon, Wellington   Tel. (04) 496.5652
                                    Telefax: (04) 496.5698

NORWAY – NORVÈGE
Narvesen Info Center – NIC
Bertrand Narvesens vei 2
P.O. Box 6125 Etterstad
0602 Oslo 6   Tel. (022) 57.33.00
                                    Telefax: (022) 68.19.01

PAKISTAN
Mirza Book Agency
65 Shahrah Quaid-E-Azam
Lahore 54000   Tel. (42) 353.601
                                    Telefax: (42) 231.730

PHILIPPINE – PHILIPPINES
International Book Center
5th Floor, Filipinas Life Bldg.
Ayala Avenue
Metro Manila   Tel. 81.96.76
                            Telex 23312 RHP PH

PORTUGAL
Livraria Portugal
Rua do Carmo 70-74
Apart. 2681
1200 Lisboa   Tel. (01) 347.49.82/5
                                    Telefax: (01) 347.02.64

SINGAPORE – SINGAPOUR
Gower Asia Pacific Pte Ltd.
Golden Wheel Building
41, Kallang Pudding Road, No. 04-03
Singapore 1334   Tel. 741.5166
                                    Telefax: 742.9356

SPAIN – ESPAGNE
Mundi-Prensa Libros S.A.
Castelló 37, Apartado 1223
Madrid 28001   Tel. (91) 431.33.99
                                    Telefax: (91) 575.39.98

Libreria Internacional AEDOS
Consejo de Ciento 391
08009 – Barcelona   Tel. (93) 488.30.09
                                    Telefax: (93) 487.76.59

Llibreria de la Generalitat
Palau Moja
Rambla dels Estudis, 118
08002 – Barcelona
                    (Subscripcions) Tel. (93) 318.80.12
                    (Publicacions) Tel. (93) 302.67.23
                                    Telefax: (93) 412.18.54

SRI LANKA
Centre for Policy Research
c/o Colombo Agencies Ltd.
No. 300-304, Galle Road
Colombo 3   Tel. (1) 574240, 573551-2
                            Telefax: (1) 575394, 510711

SWEDEN – SUÈDE
Fritzes Customer Service
S–106 47 Stockholm   Tel. (08) 690.90.90
                                    Telefax: (08) 20.50.21

Subscription Agency/Agence d'abonnements :
Wennergren-Williams Info AB
P.O. Box 1305
171 25 Solna   Tel. (08) 705.97.50
                                    Telefax: (08) 27.00.71

SWITZERLAND – SUISSE
Maditec S.A. (Books and Periodicals - Livres
et périodiques)
Chemin des Palettes 4
Case postale 266
1020 Renens VD 1   Tel. (021) 635.08.65
                                    Telefax: (021) 635.07.80

Librairie Payot S.A.
4, place Pépinet
CP 3212
1002 Lausanne   Tel. (021) 341.33.47
                                    Telefax: (021) 341.33.45

Librairie Unilivres
6, rue de Candolle
1205 Genève   Tel. (022) 320.26.23
                                    Telefax: (022) 329.73.18

Subscription Agency/Agence d'abonnements :
Dynapresse Marketing S.A.
38 avenue Vibert
1227 Carouge   Tel. (022) 308.07.89
                                    Telefax: (022) 308.07.99

See also – Voir aussi :
OECD Publications and Information Centre
August-Bebel-Allee 6
D-53175 Bonn (Germany)   Tel. (0228) 959.120
                                    Telefax: (0228) 959.12.17

THAILAND – THAÏLANDE
Suksit Siam Co. Ltd.
113, 115 Fuang Nakhon Rd.
Opp. Wat Rajbopith
Bangkok 10200   Tel. (662) 225.9531/2
                                    Telefax: (662) 222.5188

TURKEY – TURQUIE
Kültür Yayinlari Is-Türk Ltd. Sti.
Atatürk Bulvari No. 191/Kat 13
Kavaklidere/Ankara   Tel. 428.11.40 Ext. 2458
Dolmabahce Cad. No. 29
Besiktas/Istanbul   Tel. 260.71.88
                                    Telex: 43482B

UNITED KINGDOM – ROYAUME-UNI
HMSO
Gen. enquiries   Tel. (071) 873 0011
Postal orders only:
P.O. Box 276, London SW8 5DT
Personal Callers HMSO Bookshop
49 High Holborn, London WC1V 6HB
                                    Telefax: (071) 873 8200
Branches at: Belfast, Birmingham, Bristol,
Edinburgh, Manchester

UNITED STATES – ÉTATS-UNIS
OECD Publications and Information Center
2001 L Street N.W., Suite 650
Washington, D.C. 20036-4910 Tel. (202) 785.6323
                                    Telefax: (202) 785.0350

VENEZUELA
Libreria del Este
Avda F. Miranda 52, Aptdo. 60337
Edificio Galipán
Caracas 106   Tel. 951.1705/951.2307/951.1297
                            Telegram: Libreste Caracas

Subscription to OECD periodicals may also be
placed through main subscription agencies.

Les abonnements aux publications périodiques de
l'OCDE peuvent être souscrits auprès des
principales agences d'abonnement.

Orders and inquiries from countries where Distribu-
tors have not yet been appointed should be sent to:
OECD Publications Service, 2 rue André-Pascal,
75775 Paris Cedex 16, France.

Les commandes provenant de pays où l'OCDE n'a
pas encore désigné de distributeur peuvent être
adressées à : OCDE, Service des Publications,
2, rue André-Pascal, 75775 Paris Cedex 16, France.

5-1995

OECD PUBLICATIONS, 2 rue André-Pascal, 75775 PARIS CEDEX 16
PRINTED IN FRANCE
(96 95 05 1) ISBN 92-64-14430-7 - No. 47919 1995